The Complete Guide to

KENAI FJORDS

National Park, Alaska

Jim Pfeiffenberger

Greatland Graphics
Anchorage, Alaska

Lead chapter illustrations by Rockwell Kent from his book *Wilderness, A Journal of Quiet Adventure in Alaska*, originally published in 1920, courtesy of The Rockwell Kent Legacies.

Cartography: David Allen
Design: Edward Bovy
Front cover: Horned puffins, Alissa Crandall
Back cover, top to bottom:
Bear Lake and Bear Glacier, Bud Rice; Sea Lions, Chiswell Islands, and Pederson Glacier in Aialik Bay, both by Jim Pfeiffenberger

Photo copyrights retained by the photographers.

Available by mail from:
Greatland Graphics
Box 100333
Anchorage, Alaska 99510

Price: $11.95 each plus $3 per order postage and handling. Write for free catalogue of Alaska books and calendars.

The author at Exit Glacier.

Acknowledgements

I am indebted to many people who helped in the creation of this book. First of all, thanks to all of the dedicated researchers who have combined curiosity with knowledge and expertise to reveal many fascinating facts about the Kenai Fjords. Without their work and reports, my task would have been impossible.

Thanks to the following organizations for their help: The Resurrection Bay Historical Society, The Seward Community Library, the Seward Writers Group, and the Kenai Fjords National Park staff.

Thanks to the following individuals who assisted me in one way or another: Bud Rice, Linda Cook, Gail Irvine, Natalie Nadeau, Aron Crowell, Jack Sinclair, Tom Hamilton, David Hirst, Steve Nelson, Kevin McCampbell, Dot Helm, Peter Harris, Maria Gillett, Madelyn Walker, Pat Williams, Jean Schaef, Mark Luttrell, Roger MacCampbell, Linda Dubay, Tim Sczawinski, Carol Belenski and especially Susan. My sincerest apologies to anyone I have forgotten.

This book is dedicated to my father,
who showed me the beauty
of our national parks
when I was young and taught me
to love adventure.
　　　　　　　　　　　—J.P.

About the Author

Jim Pfeiffenberger has explored the Kenai Fjords extensively on foot, on skiis and by kayak. His writing and photographs have appeared in *Earth* Magazine, *Sea Kayaker*, *Aboard* Magazine, the *Anchorage Daily News* and *Bird Watcher's Digest*. He lives in Seward, Alaska.

CONTENTS

Introduction

INSIDE KENAI FJORDS

1. Where the Mountains Fall into the Sea

2. Life Finds a Foothold
   The Coastal Waters
   Plant Communities
   The Intertidal Zone
   The Coastal Forest
   AlpineTundra

3. The People Left Behind and the People Who Stayed
   Alutiiq Culture
   Russian Period
   American Period
   The Establishment of the Park
   The Oil Spill

4. Exploring Kenai Fjords

OUTSIDE KENAI FJORDS

5. Seward

6. Resurrection Bay
   Alaska State Marine Parks
   Caines Head State Recreation Area
   Alaska Maritime Wildlife Refuge

7. Kachemak Bay State Park and
Kachemak Bay State Wilderness Park

8. Appendices
   Mammal List
   Plant List
   Bird List
   Bibliography

"Resurrection Bay, Alaska" by Rockwell Kent, oil on canvas (portion).
Bear Glacier valley is depicted beyond the pod of orcas.

A Young, Raw Place

dynamic \(') di 'namik\ adj [from Greek dynamikos powerful, from dynamis power] of or relating to power, relating to physical force or energy. of or relating to forces producing physical motion. ACTIVE. characterized by continuous change or tending to produce change. FORCEFUL ENERGETIC.

—adapted from Webster's *Third New International Dictionary*

THE SILENCE IS BROKEN by a sharp crack, like a shot fired, as the movement begins. The crack is followed by a low rumble that grows and builds into a thundering roar as tons of ice collapse, as if in slow motion, into the sea. We shift and stroke gently to turn our bows into the oncoming swell. Kittiwakes reel and dive in the wake of the crashing ice, feeding on the tiny creatures that are stirred up by this awesome geological process. The iceberg rolls and floats away from the glacier, bobbing as it drifts our way. It will eventually melt and join the sea, ebbing and flooding, and someday evaporating into a cloud that will fall again as snow on the rugged peaks around us. There it will lie until it is buried and transformed into glacier ice, to flow and grind and carve at these fjords once again, and finally meet the sea and crash, as if in slow motion, into these frigid waters.

Natural arch in Aialik Bay. Wind, waves and weather combine to create
offshore sea stacks and natural arches like this arch in Aialilk Bay.
SUSAN PFEIFFENBERGER

Maybe some lucky kayaker will be here to watch the spectacle as we are now. Maybe the scene will look much the same as it does today. But more likely it will look entirely different.

"Dynamic" hardly seems a strong enough word to describe the everchanging world of the Kenai Fjords. It is a place where a summer rainstorm can suddenly set the cliffs alive with a hundred waterfalls that may flow for an instant and disappear. It is a place where young forests are busy reclaiming and transforming freshly revealed land. It is a place of quiet bays and inlets that were unknown two generations ago, buried in ice. It is a place where geology is not just some abstract notion on an incomprehensible time scale, but is a process visibly in motion. It is most certainly an active, energetic, powerful place.

Though the mountains and glaciers appear unmovable in their massiveness, they are not. The fjords we know today are hardly the same fjords that were paddled by the ancient Unegkurmiut people. The fjords that the Russian explorers mapped were different still. The glaciers have moved. The shoreline has dropped. This is a young, raw place where violent forces continue to shape the land. The beach that makes a good camp this summer may be transformed by a single winter storm or a brief, jolting earthquake. Take nothing for granted here—solid ice flows like water, and the mountains may move tomorrow.

All of this upheaval and violent change results in beauty. It is a beauty that, like the forces that have shaped and still grip this land, is not subtle. It is stark and awesome. It is huge and fantastic and soaring. Its beauty confronts us with jagged edges and menacing rumbles as we float here in our kayaks, small and overwhelmed. It is a frightening and powerful beauty that is not easily forgotten. Though the fjords will surely change as they have for millions of years, visions of this day will reappear in my mind, memories of a sharp crack and of ice in slow motion, memories of a colossal world changing as I look on, dreamlike memories of a dynamic, seemingly impossible beauty.

Inside Kenai Fiords

CHAPTER 1

Where the Mountains Fall into the Sea: Geology Sets the Stage

The Restless Earth

GREAT FORCES ARE AT WORK IN THIS LAND. Glaciers gouge and carve the rock. Earthquakes rattle the soaring mountains. Storms batter the shorelines. Avalanches sweep down the slopes. High mountain valleys sink and drown in the sea. Like some giant sculpture in progress, the fjords have an unfinished feel. Geological forces chip away relentlessly, shaping, changing, and reshaping this land right before our eyes.

The great evolving sculpture of the fjords began some 65 million years ago, far from the present location of the national park. In fact, most all of the rock and land bordering the Gulf of Alaska in a great arc from Southeast Alaska through the Kenai Peninsula to Kodiak Island is believed to have originated elsewhere. As the Pacific and North American plates grind together along the coast, large pieces of the continent are torn loose. The

(previous page) **Harris Bay and the entrance to Northwestern Fjord.** (left) **Recent glacial retreat has revealed scoured granite walls in Northwestern Fjord.**
AUSTIN POST/USGS ICE AND CLIMATE PROJECT

Pacific Plate, inching slowly northward, carries these shattered pieces of continent with it and redeposits them in new locations. Many of coastal Alaska's rock formations, or terranes, consist of such transplanted material. Like many of Alaska's current human residents, these terranes have essentially been uprooted from somewhere south, hitched a ride, and resettled in the north country.

The rock assemblage which comprises the bulk of the Kenai Mountains is known as the Chugach Terrane. It is composed of two geological formations. One is the McHugh Complex, which is mostly marine volcanic rock mixed with chert and shale from the late Triassic (230 million years ago) to Late Cretaceous periods (90 million years ago). These rocks were ripped up and brought northward by the drifting oceanic plate. The other formation is known as the Valdez Group, which is largely marine sedimentary rocks from the Late Cretaceous period (65 million years ago). These sandstones, shales, mudstones, and

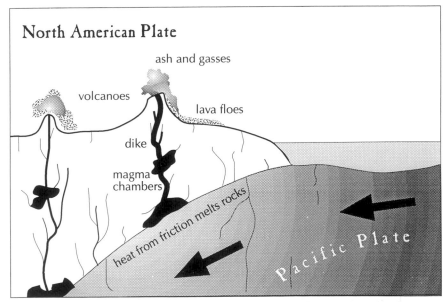

The massive collision of the Pacific and North American plates in coastal Alaska results in periodic volcanic eruptions and earth tremors and quakes.

pebble conglomerates were formed on the edge of the oceanic plate as it drifted northward. Unfortunately, they do not contain a good fossil record.

Ten million years later the another geological process began that had great influence on the shape of the fjords we see today. Deep beneath the surface of the earth, molten rock seeped slowly upward and intruded into the sedimentary layers of the Chugach Terrane. It cooled and formed a hard granite plug beneath the surface rock. Much of this rock was eventually uplifted and folded into jagged mountains. Eons of coastal Alaskan rain, snow, and glaciation washed away the softer sedimentary rock, and the granite beneath was exposed. Harder and more resistant to erosion, it forms many of the prominent features seen in the park today, such as Aialik Cape, the Harris Peninsula, many of the isolated peaks jutting out of the Harding Icefield, and the Chiswell Islands. An exposed body of intrusive granite like this is called a batholith; this particular one is known as the Harding Icefield batholith. The chemical composition of the Harding Icefield batholith is nearly identical to the sedimentary rocks of the Valdez Group, suggesting that it formed from melted portions of the Chugach Terrane itself.

The Kenai Peninsula lies near the edge of the North American continental plate. Not far offshore, the Pacific Plate and the North American Plate grind together in a slow motion collision. The area where this collision takes place is known as a subduction zone, and it is here that, over time, the Pacific Plate is forced beneath the continent, or subducted. The results of this grinding and subduction are manyfold. For example, just as rubbing your hands together generates heat, the rubbing of the plates generates great amounts of heat. It was this friction heat that melted the rock that eventually oozed upward and formed the Harding Icefield batholith. Also, as the Pacific Plate is forced down, the edge of the continental plate is crumpled and compressed, resulting in folded, uplifted coastal mountains. The Kenai Mountains, like many coastal mountain ranges, are the product of a huge geological collision taking place just offshore. This collision continues today, making southcentral Alaska and the Kenai Fjords among the most seismically active areas in the world.

All of the processes described so far—the accretion of the terranes, the emplacement of the Harding Icefield batholith, and the uplift of the Kenai Mountains—can be thought of as a sort of gathering of materials and rough shaping work. The finer sculpting and details of the landscape were left to the glaciers.

Two-and-a-half million years ago, the temperatures around the world began to gradually drop. This meant that snow fell earlier each fall and persisted later into each spring. At higher elevations, the snow remained year round, and year after year it piled up, high and deep. Under the pressure of its own weight, the snow was compacted and transformed into masses of ice that began to creep slowly downhill. In high mountain ranges the world over, glaciers were born. In polar regions where glaciers already existed, the glaciers grew and expanded. The earth was gripped by the icy hand of the Pleistocene Ice Age.

In the Kenai Mountains, where the storms swept in from the ancient sea, the snow piled up so high and deep that a massive icefield was formed that fed glaciers flowing out in all directions. All but the highest peaks were buried by a barren expanse of ice. The glaciers plowed down through the mountains like slow, unstoppable bulldozers, carving cirques, piling up moraines, and gouging deep, wide U-shaped valleys where V-shaped river valleys had existed before. The fjords as we know them began to take shape.

There were many periods of glacial advance during the Pleistocene which were interrupted by warmer, "interglacial" periods. The glaciers of the Kenai Mountains melted and shrunk during these warm periods, only to move forward once again when temperatures dropped. The last major glaciation in southern Alaska during the Pleistocene Ice Age took place around 24,000 to 10,000 years ago, during what's referred to as the Late

PRINCIPAL ROCK TYPES OF KENAI FJORDS

Graywacke A gray colored sedimentary rock called sandstone. Graywacke from the Late Cretaceous Period makes up the bulk of the Kenai Mountains.

Shale A finer grained sedimentary rock. Also from the Late Cretaceous Period in Kenai Fjords.

Granite and **Granodiorite** Intrusive igneous rock from the Tertiary Period that forms Harris Peninsula, Aialik Cape, Chiswell Islands and some of the nunataks on the Harding Icefield.

Other rock types found in the Park include quartz, greenstone, slate, tuff, conglomerate, and chert.

Wisconsin. During the Late Wisconsin, the Harding Icefield expanded to the north and west. The fjords were not filled with seawater but were practically buried under grinding blue ice. The Resurrection River Valley was completely filled with hundreds of feet of snow and ice that extended far out into what is now Resurrection Bay. A huge, flat glacier occupied the Kenai Peninsula lowlands and Cook Inlet. The land we know as beautiful and abundant today was an inhospitable frozen wasteland.

As global temperatures warmed, the great ice sheets melted back, but didn't disappear completely. The Harding Icefield is one of the remnants. It has persisted for tens of thousands of years and continues to feed enormous glaciers today. Over seven hundred square miles are still covered by this frigid glacial blanket. No accurate measure of its thickness has ever been made, though it is certainly hundreds and perhaps even thousands of feet deep. Though the Kenai Mountains are not all that high, nor are the temperatures here particularly cold, the tremendous amount of snowfall that sweeps in from the Gulf of Alaska continues to replenish this Pleistocene landscape. The barren plain of snow is interrupted only occasionally by island-like peaks known as "nunataks." Gazing out over this vast sea of ice is like looking back in time. Much of North America was once inundated like this.

The Great Quake

Seismic activity is the other major force that has been at work for thousands of years on this grand sculpture. Earthquakes continue to rattle the Kenai Peninsula regularly, and, along with the glaciers, have had a big part in shaping the bays and coves of the Kenai Fjords. As the Pacific Oceanic Plate and the North American Plate push together just offshore, great pressure builds up. This pressure is occasionally relieved when rocks deep within the earth give way or rearrange themselves. These rearrangements once caused the uplift of the Kenai Mountains. Today, they are causing these same mountains to sink slowly into the sea.

Wherever tectonic plates collide, one is forced beneath the other. In southern Alaska, the Pacific Oceanic Plate, made of dense, heavy material, dives beneath the less dense North American Plate. The edge of the North American Plate is bent and dragged down in the process, in essence sticking to the Pacific Plate as it dives. The Kenai Mountains, lying near the edge of the North American Plate, are dragged down with each successive earthquake. The result is that glacial features such as cirques and U-shaped valleys which were formed in the mountains well above sea level are now submerged and form beautifully sculpted coves, bays and fjords. The Aialik Peninsula is one of the best examples of this "drowning mountain range" phenomenon anywhere in the world.

On March 27, 1964, the largest earthquake ever recorded

struck southern Alaska, dropping the Kenai Fjords coastline as much as six feet in just a few minutes of shaking. Beaches fell into the sea, forests were inundated with salt water, huge rockslides littered the glaciers, and ice avalanches plummeted down the steep fjord walls.

After the rumbling stopped, the coasts were slammed by a series of gigantic waves. Tsunamis (earthquake-generated waves), seiches (waves caused by sloshing motion in the bays), and waves generated locally by underwater landslides all combined to devastate the shorelines. Driftwood and rocks were hurled violently into the forests, smashing into living trees and leaving scars that can still be found today. Scores of rotting trees that died when the quake lowered their roots into saltwater still line the shores. These eerie "ghost forests" stand as mute testament to the continuing geological processes at work in the Kenai Fjords.

Alaska Railroad tracks bent by the 1964 quake, 37 miles north of Seward.
ANCHORAGE MUSEUM OF HISTORY AND ART/ALASKA RAILROAD COLLECTION BL79.2.4744, H. BJERKE PHOTOGRAPHER

THE CLUES OF A GLACIER'S PAST

To understand the history of a glacier's past advances and re-treats, a glacial geologist must rely on a variety of clues. The direct geological evidence of a glacier's movement, such as obvious moraines or trimlines, is combined with less direct botanical clues. For example, trees growing on an old end moraine are cored, then the growth rings counted. If the oldest tree found is 100 years old, glaciologists know that the glacier withdrew from this spot at least 100 years ago.

On clean, exposed bedrock where trees won't grow, lichens with known growth rates are measured and aged. The growth rates of certain lichens were first discovered in graveyards where they grow on tombstones that have exact dates on them for reference. In the Kenai Fjords region, historical features such as old mine dumps also help determine lichen growth rates.

In some cases, as glaciers pushed forward, they plowed over trees and buried their stumps in icy gravel, where they were preserved for centuries. Erosion has re-exposed some of this ancient wood today, and it can be radiocarbon dated. Single bits of ancient wood have been found near glaciers in Kenai Fjords dating back to 1500 BC, and entire "forests" of stumps dating back to around 900 AD have been discovered. Such "forests" are clear evidence that an area was not covered by ice at the time the trees grew. The growth rings of these ancient trees also provide important clues about climate and glacial advance in the ancient environment of Kenai Fjords.

Glacial retreat and subsequent erosion has exposed stumps from ancient forests in some parts of the fjords. / BUD RICE

Northwestern Fjord

BUD RICE

THE FORMATION OF THE FJORDS

A fjord is defined as a long, narrow, deep arm of the sea filling a once-glaciated coastal mountain valley. The formation of the Kenai Fjords began millions of years ago when V-shaped river valleys were eroded in the ancient Kenai Mountains. With the onset of the ice age, glaciers formed in the mountains and flowed down these existing valleys, gouging and widening them into steep, parabola-shaped trenches. In many cases, these trenches were deepened to below sea level.

When the glaciers receded, the sea invaded these widened valleys, forming the fjords we see today. The melting of the massive ice age glaciers added so much water to the world's oceans that sea level rose, adding further to the inundation of these coastal valleys.

The subduction of the North American plate along the edge of the Kenai Peninsula continues to drown the fjords today. Millions of years from now, the entire Kenai mountain range could lie beneath the sea.

DEVELOPMENT OF A FJORD

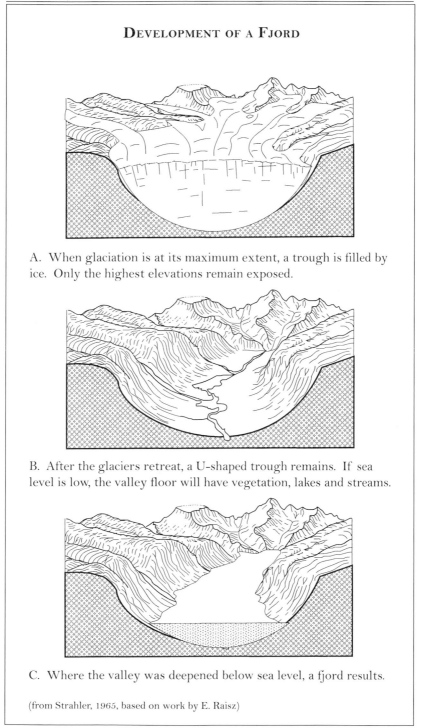

A. When glaciation is at its maximum extent, a trough is filled by ice. Only the highest elevations remain exposed.

B. After the glaciers retreat, a U-shaped trough remains. If sea level is low, the valley floor will have vegetation, lakes and streams.

C. Where the valley was deepened below sea level, a fjord results.

(from Strahler, 1965, based on work by E. Raisz)

The Glaciers at Work Today

The work of the glaciers is continuing today. Since the Late Wisconsin, there have been other, smaller glacial advances in the Kenai Mountains that have had big effects on what we see in the park today. Recent movements have scoured the mountain walls, piled rocks and sediment here and there, and reshaped the fjord bottoms. Glaciologists have interpreted a number of clues in an attempt to understand these most recent events in the ongoing sculpture of the fjords.

Many of the glaciers in the Kenai Mountains apparently made an advance that began around 400 to 500 AD and continued for some 200 years. When global temperatures rose, they retreated for several hundred years. The so-called "Little Ice Age," the last world-wide expansion of glaciers, lasted from around 1300 AD into the 1890s. Evidence suggests that McCarty and Aialik glaciers advanced perhaps as early as 900 AD, and were followed by the others a few centuries later. By a series of fits and starts, the glaciers of Kenai Fjords reached their most advanced Little Ice Age positions in the late 1800s and early 1900s. The glaciers have been mostly retreating since then.

Exit Glacier

Exit Glacier today is a steep tongue of ice that drops 2500 feet from the Harding Icefield in just three miles. The ice flows downhill fairly swiftly, averaging 20 inches per day. Though the glacier appears to have been shrinking for decades, recent studies show net gains in the past few years and suggest that Exit Glacier may once again be moving forward.

Radiocarbon dates from preserved wood samples indicate that Exit Glacier began its last big advance sometime around the mid 1600s. It plowed down the valley to a point nearly two

Ghost forest in Quicksand Cove, Aialik Bay. / Jim Pfeiffenberger miles beyond its present terminus, reaching its most recent maximum position by the early 1800s. It was sometime soon after 1825 that it began its long retreat to its current position.

Each time the glacier paused in its retreat, it deposited another pile of debris, or end moraine, before continuing to shrink back. Today, there are a series of six concentric moraines that were left behind as Exit Glacier withdrew up the valley over the past hundred and seventy-five years. The most recent of these moraines is clearly visible as you stand in front of the glacier and look down the valley. The sparsely vegetated piles of gravel, rocks, and sand just on the other side of the creek mark the glacier's position in 1950. Older moraines can be spotted along the road between the parking lot and the bridge—look for small, abrupt hills in the otherwise flat floor of the cottonwood forest. You can be sure that just about anywhere you walk or drive in the immediate Exit Glacier area was buried under ice in the not-so-distant past. You are traveling a fresh, new landscape here, one that was only recently freed from ice, and one that may again be consumed by it.

Glaciers of Aialik Bay

Three major glaciers spill down from the Harding Icefield into Aialik Bay. Two of these, Holgate and Aialik glaciers, flow to tidewater, while the third, Pederson Glacier, ends at a lake less than a mile from the ocean. These three rivers of jagged, shattered ice, and their associated icebergs, make for some of the most beautiful scenery in the park.

At the head of the bay lies the massive, sparkling Aialik Glacier. This glacier calves enormous icebergs into the bay that become resting places for seals and sea otters. The glacier's terminus has been at its current location since at least 1909, when Aialik Bay was first surveyed by geologists, and perhaps since the mid-19th century. Maps from this period show no indication of an advanced position. There *is* an indication of an

Some Common Questions About Exit Glacier

Why is the glacier blue?
 When sunlight travels through the ice, it is bent, or refracted, and
 separated into all of the colors of the rainbow, much like light pass-
 ing through a prism. The glacier ice, though, is not smooth and
 clear like a prism. There are many jagged crystal edges, air bubbles,
 and bits of trapped debris in the ice. Therefore, the light is bent
 over and over again as is passes through this uneven mix of surfaces. Energy is absorbed every time the light is bent. Only the
 highest energy wavelengths pass completely through—all the rest
 are absorbed. Since blue is the highest energy wavelength of visible light, it passes through, and the glacier looks blue.

How fast does the ice flow downhill?
 Studies conducted in 1985 by National Park Service personnel in-
 dicated that the ice flows downhill about 20 inches, or nearly two
 feet per day.

**If the ice is flowing downhill that much, why doesn't the glacier
get two feet longer every day?**
 The ice is also melting, eroding, and evaporating as it flows downhill. If less than two feet per day melts, then the glacier does get
 longer and it pushes forward. Exit Glacier usually pushes forward
 some each winter when melting is minimal. If two feet per day
 melts, then the glacier's terminus stays more or less in one place.
 If more than two feet per day melts, the glacier gets shorter, or
 recedes, and the terminus "moves" back. A receding glacier is not
 really moving uphill—it is simply losing more ice to melting than
 winter snowfall and downhill flow are adding, thus it gets shorter.
 Exit Glacier usually recedes some each summer, when melting is
 greatest. In recent years, forward winter movement has outpaced
 summer melting, and Exit Glacier has grown slightly longer over-
 all.

How old is the ice?
 At two feet per day, it takes ice approximately thirty years to flow
 down the entire three-and-a-half-mile length of Exit Glacier. Some
 of the ice may be coming from deep within the Harding Icefield
 and could be even older.

advanced position in the fjord itself—a submerged terminal moraine that runs across the bay some five miles south of the current face of Aialik Glacier. Little is known about the glacier's advance to this spot. Radiocarbon and tree-ring dating suggest that it reached this maximum position sometime between 1100 AD and 1600 AD, but further study is needed to narrow the range to a more specific date.

Holgate Glacier is similarly mysterious. A submerged moraine at the entrance to Holgate Arm clearly indicates that the glacier once terminated there, over three miles from where it meets the sea now. Tree ring counts show that the middle of Holgate Arm has been ice free since at least 1663 AD. It is possible that Holgate Glacier extended all the way to the moraine when the Pilgrims stepped ashore at Plymouth Rock, but it must certainly have been in retreat soon after.

Pederson Glacier shows a more complete picture of position change and retreat over the last hundred years. When it was first surveyed in 1909, a portion of the face came all the way to tidewater and calved directly into the fjord. Since then, it has retreated nearly a mile to its present position. A series of six moraines has been identified and dated, indicating that Pederson reached its Little Ice Age maximum around the 1885.

Northwestern Fjord

The glaciers of Northwestern Fjord have been in dramatic retreat for much of this century. The entrance to the fjord is marked by a shallow moraine which is largely exposed at low tide and makes boating in the area a tricky proposition. The glacier stretched all the way to this moraine in the late 1800s, filling the entire lagoon that we know today. The retreat of this mega-glacier has been constant since the turn of the century. Maps from 1950 show the ice front six miles back from the mo-

Holgate Glacier / Austin Post/USGS Ice and Climate Project

raine, and since then, Northwestern Glacier has retreated another three-and-a-half miles. Recent observations show that the
steep ice curtains still clinging to the mountain walls continue
to melt and thin. This shrinking back of the ice has revealed a
beautiful fjord of polished granite islands and smooth, protected
waters. Close to the glaciers, the vegetation gives way to bare,
scoured rock rising from the cold depths. The constant crashing of the ice and the pervasive piles of debris give this place the
feel of a giant construction yard. This is a work in progress. It
is a raw, naked landscape stripped down to its elements—rock,
water and ice.

McCarty Fjord

McCarty Fjord is a straight, steep-sided, 21-mile-long bay
which ends at McCarty Glacier. The last 14 miles of navigable
salt water were occupied by ice at the turn of the century. Like
Northwestern Glacier, McCarty has been in dramatic retreat for
nearly the last hundred years. The upper section of this fjord is
surrounded by new land, and the barren valleys and rocky walls
have just begun to come alive with fireweed and alder thickets in
the wake of the recent thaw.

The geological record shows that McCarty Glacier has been
repeatedly advancing and retreating over the last three thousand years. The presence of extensive buried forests in the upper fjord have allowed researchers to develop a detailed chronology of the glacier's movements since the 6th century as it
pulsed back and forth in the fjord. A series of major advances
finally found the terminus just outside of James lagoon in 1905,
nearly 15 miles from its current position. A submerged moraine
clearly marks this advance.

At some point after 1910, the glacier lost contact with this
moraine, and the dramatic retreat began. Icebergs thundered
off the mass faster than it could feed itself from the icefield above,
and it withdrew rapidly up the fjord, revealing a deep upper ba-

sin. It took just 55 years for McCarty Glacier to reach its current position, where it has held more or less steady since the
early 60s, with some slight gains. Will it push ahead once again,
scouring away the forests in its path? Or will it shrink back into
the mountains, freeing more water and land from its icy grip?
Until more is known about glacial dynamics, we can only sit
back and watch as the ice displays its awesome power and continues to shape the fjords before our eyes.

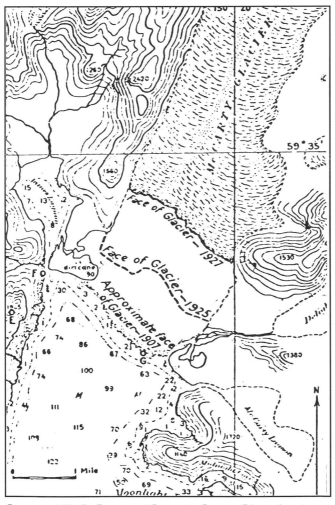

**Section of U. S. Coast and Geodetic Survey Chart showing
retreat of McCarty Glacier as of 1927.** / U. S. Geological Survey

ICEWORMS

There is only one creature known that spends its entire life on frigid glaciers—the iceworm. These tiny black worms are cousins to the common earthworm, but rather than burrowing into dirt, they wriggle down among ice and snow granules to eke out their cold existence. They prefer to live at a constant 32 degrees F. Just a few degrees colder and they freeze solid. A bit warmer and they can't take the heat—they die and disintegrate at 40 degrees F. In the top layers of snow and ice, they find a 32-degree world that is insulated from extreme winter cold and summertime heat. They also find the food that sustains their 3/4-inch-long bodies—windblown pollen and algae. Tiny bristles called *setae* on the iceworm's skin allow it to maneuver through this slippery environment of ice.

You might see iceworms by hiking to the end of the Harding Icefield trail and searching the permanent snowfields there. It's best to search in the evening since iceworms shun the sun and disappear deep into the snow during midday. The best opportunity for seeing them is on the icefield itself, but this should only be attempted by experienced mountaineers with ropes, harnesses, anchors and glacial travel experience. You may see hundreds of them inching along in search of pollen. When near the surface like this, they make easy prey for alpine songbirds such as snow buntings and rosy finches.

BUD RICE

GLACIERS

Often described as "rivers of ice," glaciers are dynamic structures that move and flow downhill. They can form wherever winter snow-fall exceeds the summer melt for many years in a row. The surplus snow is slowly changed into ice by a combination of pressure, melting, and refreezing.

Once the ice mass grows large enough, it begins to flow down-hill, slow and thick like molasses, under the force of gravity and the pressure of its own weight. This flowing ice has tremendous power to change landscapes.

Glaciers push tons of loose rock in front of them like bulldozers. They also transport rocks on their surfaces like conveyor belts. Huge boulders, called erratics, often end up miles from their original loca-tions by hitching rides on glaciers. Pebbles and other debris are trapped and dragged along the beneath the ice, scratching and gouging into the bedrock surface.

All of this moving ice and rock widens valleys into steep, U-shaped troughs. If these troughs happen to be in coastal areas, they may fill with sea water when the glaciers recede, creating fjords. Glaciers are active sculptors on a huge, geological scale.

(above) The retreat of Bear Glacier is forming Bear Lake. The lake is protected from the sea by a small gravel beach.

(left) Drowned cirques at the head of the Aialik Peninsula. Aialik Bay and Pederson (l) and Aialik (r) glaciers in the background. / SUSAN PFEIFFENBERGER

THE EXPLORATION OF THE HARDING ICEFIELD

Though the Natives certainly knew it was there, the Harding Icefield was first recognized and described by modern geologists in 1915 when C.G. Martin, B.L.Johnson, and U.S. Grant published their report, "Geology and Mineral Resources of Kenai Peninsula, Alaska." A young cartographer named Rufus Sargent had done the actual surveying and mapping of the area, and another large icefield northeast of the Harding bears his name today.

In 1936, a young Swiss adventurer named Yul Kilcher found himself stuck in Seward waiting on a steamer to take him to Homer. He grew impatient, and after a few days finally set off on foot. After a long struggle up the steep, heavily wooded slopes, he finally came out on the flat, open expanse of the icefield, where he promptly fell into a glacial crevasse and nearly vanished. His backpack caught in the snow, though, and spared him an icy grave. Pulling himself up from the edge of the abyss, he continued on until a mixed rain and snow storm pinned him down in a whiteout. When the skies finally cleared, he was unable to determine his location and deemed it wisest to follow his tracks back to Seward. This was the first known attempt to cross the Harding Icefield on foot.

The feat was not achieved until 41 years later, when a party led by mountaineer Vin Hoeman completed a crossing from Homer to Seward on skis and snowshoes in 1967. They "exited" the icefield on a small glacier northwest of Seward, today known as Exit Glacier. Yul Kilcher was a member of this party, and remembers being received like a hero in Seward. The traverse has since been completed on numerous occasions, though many groups are still turned back by fierce storms of the sort that stopped Kilcher in 1936.

Harding Icefield and the Gulf of Alaska beyond. / Susan Pfeiffenberger

Glacier Terms

crevass Deep open fracture in the surface of a glacier

end moraine Distinct accumulation of rocky material at the end of a glacier

erratic Large rock fragment transported and deposited by a glacier

fjord A long, narrow, deep arm of the sea filling a glaciated coastal mountain valley

glacier A body of natural, land-borne ice that flows

icefield A sheet of glacier ice that collects in a mountain range or between adjoining ranges and generally flows out radially

moraine A ridge of stony debris built by transport of rock and sediment by glacial ice

nunatak An Eskimo word meaning "lonely peak," it is used by glaciologists today to describe any island of bedrock projecting above a surrounding mass of glacier ice

striations Linear, fine parallel scratches cut into a rock surface by debris carried at the base of a glacier

terminal moraine Outermost end moraine deposited during a major episode of glacial advance

trimline Sharp line between vegetated and unvegetated terrain, or between older and younger vegetation, marking the limit of recent glacial advance.

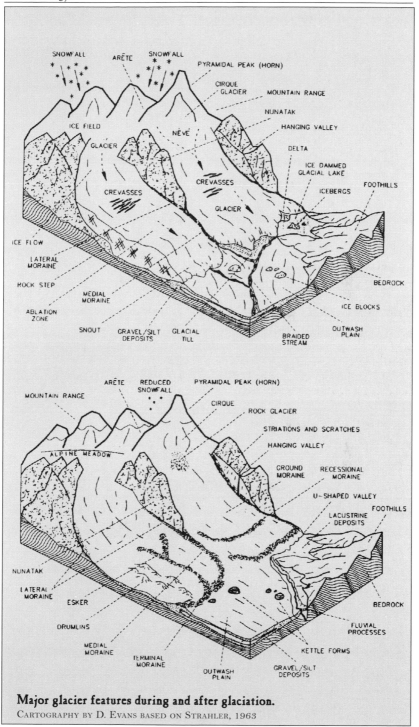

Major glacier features during and after glaciation.

Cartography by D. Evans based on Strahler, 1963

CHAPTER 2

Life Finds a Foothold:
Flora and Fauna Colonize the New Land

THE VAST MAJORITY OF KENAI FJORDS National Park is composed of snow, ice and bare rock. The narrow band of ice free coastline is mostly steep, inhospitable terrain. It is snow covered for much of the year, regularly blasted by fierce winds and scoured by frequent avalanches. Survival is difficult but life, with its patient adaptation and mysterious tenacity, has managed to find a foothold here.

From the glacier's edge, where windswept boulders are splattered with slow-growing lichens, to the lush spruce forests, where the footfalls of the black bear are muffled by a thick carpet of moss, from the lonely summits of nunataks, where tiny flowers poke their blossoms skyward for a few short weeks, to the rocky tidepools where fish and crabs carry on year round in the nourishing surge, life has slowly but surely blanketed whatever land has been freed from the ice.

The plants and animals of Kenai Fjords don't merely sur-

Rock ptarmigan / BUD RICE

vive in this harsh environment—they thrive. Whales spout and play in the fertile offshore waters. Wolverines roam from beach to ridgetop. Coyotes, weasels and bears wander the forest, and salmon choke the streams each summer. Tens of thousands of seabirds choose to raise their young here. Despite the apparent severity of this icy landscape, Kenai Fjords harbors a rich array of complex, intertwined ecosystems.

The Coastal Waters

The cold coastal waters that fill the fjords teem with life each summer. The long hours of sunlight encourage huge blooms of phytoplankton, a basic building block of ocean food chains. Winds and currents combine to create a nearshore upwelling of nutrient-rich water. Since cold water holds more oxygen than warm water, fish and other creatures thrive here. This concentration of life in the summer sea supports local populations of seals, sea otters and sea lions, and attracts distant wanderers like 35-ton gray whales and flocks of migratory seabirds. Thousands of salmon return each summer and fall, spawning in the swift, clear streams. These creatures are tangled together in intricate and little understood food webs as the icy fingers of the Gulf of Alaska become a nourishing, living soup, a lively broth fed upon by humans and animals alike.

Whales. Several species of whales inhabit the fjords, some year-round and some for just the summer months. The most conspicuous of these are the humpback whales and the orcas. Humpbacks are summertime migrants, travelling from distant breeding grounds in Hawaii to feed on the bounty in the fjords. These huge creatures, reaching lengths of fifty feet and weights of exceeding 70,000 pounds, feed on some of the smallest creatures in the sea—tiny, shrimp-like krill and small schooling fish. They sometimes feed together, using a fascinating technique called "bubble-netting" to catch their prey. One whale dives deep beneath a school of fish and then swims in a circle, releasing bubbles from its blowhole. The rising bubbles form a cylindrical "net" in the water through which the fish will not pass. The whales then charge up through the net with their mouths open and swallow their prey. They also feed by gulping mouthfuls of seawater, then forcing this cold, salty "soup" through their baleen plates, filtering out krill and other organisms.

Humpbacks are one of the most acrobatic of the large whales, often leaping skyward in a spectacular display known as *breaching*. They also tend to congregate near shore on both their summer feeding grounds and their winter breeding grounds. This made them easy targets for the whalers of the late nineteenth and early twentieth centuries. There may have been as many as 15,000 humpbacks in the North Pacific prior to commercial whaling. By the time they received full international protection in 1964, less than 1,000 were left. Recovery has been slow, and they are still listed as endangered today.

Orcas, or killer whales, are the other species most likely to be encountered in the fjords. They are social animals that often travel in family *pods* of a dozen or more whales, feeding on fish and sometimes other marine mammals. The males can be recognized by their tall black dorsal fins—these are small animals compared to the humpbacks, weighing in at a mere six-to-eight tons. Orcas navigate and communicate by emitting a series of clicks, groans and weird squeals. Kayakers or boaters can drop an underwater microphone overboard and listen in on these mysterious conversations as the whales pass by. The orcas are year-round residents of the Gulf of Alaska and recent studies indicate that some of the whales that frequent the fjords also travel to Prince William Sound and Kodiak Island waters.

Other whales that are seen in the Kenai Fjords area occasionally include gray whales, fin whales, minke whales, and sei whales.

Steller's Sea Lions. Steller's sea lions regularly patrol the waters of the fjords, searching for fish to fill their bellies. Named for naturalist G.W. Steller who travelled to Alaska in 1741 with Vitus Bering, they are easy to tell from seals by their chocolate brown color, bulging eyes, and large size. Adult females typically weigh around 600 pounds, the males 1,200 pounds or more. They use the smooth granite shelves of the Chiswell Islands as resting places, or *haulouts*. You may see huge, battle-scarred bulls rocking to and fro on their flippers, females with pups relaxing in the sun, or juveniles cavorting in the nearby water. The haulouts are a constant hub-bub of moaning, belching, snoring, shifting, quivering sea lion flesh.

Unfortunately, all is not well with the Steller's sea lions these days. Their numbers in the North Pacific, including the Kenai Fjords area, are rapidly dwindling. The cause for their decline remains a mystery. Recent studies show that pups are still be-

Sea lions rest or "haul out" on a rock beach in the Chiswell Islands.
JIM PFEIFFENBERGER

ing produced at most rookeries, but that fewer are surviving to adulthood. Those that do survive are smaller than the sea lions of a decade ago. They were recently listed as a threatened species and may soon be designated endangered.

Harbor Seals. Harbor seals tend to congregate near the tidewater glaciers of the fjords where they haul out on the icebergs to rest and bear their young. They are relatively safe from predators here, though orcas will occasionally enter the icepack to hunt them. Fattened on a diet of fish, octopus and squid, harbor seals grow from 24 pounds at birth to around 200 pounds as adults. They are known to follow fish up streams and rivers and have been seen in Addison Lake near Pederson Glacier.

Sea Otters. The sea otter is the smallest of all marine mammals, with the largest adults weighing around 100 pounds. They lack the fatty blubber layer that insulates most marine mammals from the cold sea, having instead a thick fur that holds in their heat. They can have up to 650,000 individual hairs in one square inch of pelt. This luxurious coat, which ensures their survival, must be constantly groomed and cleaned—the playful-looking antics that sea otters are so well loved for are actually an important part of maintaining their insulation. This rich coat was also nearly the cause of their extinction. Sea otter fur was once the most valuable on Asian markets, and the Russians and Americans hunted them mercilessly in the 18th, 19th and early 20th centuries. The sea otter has made a steady comeback since hunting was banned in 1911, and today their population may be as large as it was in pre-hunting days.

The presence or absence of sea otters from a nearshore coastal community can have a profound effect on the makeup of the community. They feed on a variety of shellfish, particularly sea urchins and others that graze on marine plants. Where there are no sea otters, grazers may dominate the community and keep kelp and seaweed growth at a minimum. Where sea otters feed, though, grazers are kept in check and lush kelp forests often develop. The kelp forest is a more productive environment than one dominated by grazing urchins, as many marine species thrive in its cover. Sea otters in Kenai Fjords are most abundant in Northwestern Lagoon and McCarty Fjord, where submerged glacial moraines create healthy shallow feeding grounds. They may also be occasionally seen hauled out next to seals on icebergs near tidewater glaciers.

Seabirds. Many of the seabirds that breed along the park's coast are related members of one family, the alcids. Horned and tufted puffins, common and thick-billed murres, marbled and Kittlittz's murrelets, rhinoceros and parakeet auklets, and pigeon guillemots are all alcids, a family sometimes called "the penguins of the north." Though unrelated to penguins, alcids fill the same ecological niche as the penguins do in southern waters—they are diving birds that pursue fish underwater by

Black oystercatcher eggs

BUD RICE

Black-legged kittiwakes

swimming with strong wingbeats. Unlike penguins, alcids can fly, but their wings are stubby and their flight weak. They are just as likely to dive underwater to escape threats as they are to fly. Given a few more thousand years of evolution, some alcids may end up as flightless as penguins are today.

There are also prolific colonies of black-legged kittiwakes, glaucous winged gulls, and pelagic and red-faced cormorants along the park's coastline. Many of these birds begin gathering on their breeding grounds as early as March and the colonies are in full swing by late May. A cruise through the Chiswell Islands will reveal hundreds of puffins buzzing overhead while kittwakes chatter and flit around their cliffside nests. Common murres line the ledges, standing patiently as if waiting for something to happen. If that something turns out to be a bald eagle soaring past, hundreds of birds will hit the air with a communal scream to ward off the predator. Peregrine falcons also make the Chiswells home, swooping down to feed on their unsuspecting neighbors. Until late August, the colonies are constantly abuzz with the business of hatching, raising, and fledging the next generation. By fall, though, the puffins and murres are out to sea, the kittiwakes are fledged and gone, and the cliffs fall silent for the long winter.

Plant Communities

The vegetation that blankets the shores and mountains of Kenai Fjords is commonly divided into zones—the intertidal, the coastal forest and the alpine tundra. While these zones have many unique qualities that separate them from one another, there also are connections that combine them into one continuous tapestry of life. Lupine and fireweed that grow on cobble beaches at tideline are also found clinging in stunted form to the rocky nunataks of the Harding Icefield. Berries that ripen in the shade of spruce forests have near cousins in the open alpine expanses. Black bears, nourished at seaside on spawning salmon, lumber up to the high country to gobble berries, their trails like threads that sew together the fabric of these varied lifezones. They carry with them the energy of the sea and the forest, which they digest and drop in the tundra—rich fertilizer for the thin alpine soils. A mountain goat, fattened on alpine grasses, may fall victim to a winter avalanche and be swept down to the beach where its body will be devoured by hungry scavengers—a raven, a wolverine, a coyote or an eagle. A stream born in the high mountains will gather minerals on its way to the sea and sprinkle them through the intertidal community. Thus while the various zones appear distinct to us, the energy that flows through them joins them in a thousand subtle ways, and the closer we look, the less distinct the boundaries are.

The Intertidal Zone

The "edge effect" is a phenomenon referred to by biologists and ecologists to describe certain particularly rich life zones. The theory is that along the edge where two major environments meet, a greater variety of habitats exist, resulting in a more diverse assortment of organisms—a richer life zone. This enhanced biological diversity is found along all sorts of edges—where a forest meets a clearing, where a wetland meets a meadow, or where a river cuts through a prairie. There is perhaps no more obvious edge, though, than where the land meets the sea. Two fundamentally different environments come together here, one characterized by fresh water, a gaseous atmosphere, and great temperature fluctuation, the other a relatively constant world of salt water. In Kenai Fjords National Park, where the mountains fall into the sea, this blending of two worlds results in a fascinating intertidal zone that is just beginning to be understood.

There are two sets of tides per day along the Kenai Peninsula coast, that is, two high tides and two low tides per day. The difference between the highest highs and the lowest lows can be as much as 17 feet in the fjords. This continual ebb and flow results in constant variation in the moisture, salinity, temperature, and nutrient availability of the intertidal zone. The plants and animals living there have adapted to survive these variations, many with abilities to close up tightly and preserve moisture when the tide goes out. More importantly, the exchange of the tides is not always a gentle affair. Winds and currents conspire to create powerful waves and strong surges that threaten to wash the shores clean. The intertidal organisms must concern themselves with staying put and have developed a variety of methods including strong *holdfasts* that anchor plants to the rocks, flexible stalks that resist tearing, chemical bonding of shell to rock, strong muscular "feet" for holding on, and dense clustering of organisms.

The intertidal zone itself is divided into several zones that tend to form distinct bands of organisms. These bands result from varying distribution of predators, competition for space, differing abilities to survive exposure to air, and other factors yet to be fully understood.   The exact composition of these bands may differ from one location to the next based many variables—wave action, proximity of freshwater outlets, presence of bird colonies, or slope of the shore. The highest and lowest zones tend to be the most uniform, while the middle zones can show great variation. Nonetheless, a general model of zonation in the northwest Gulf of Alaska (adapted from *The Exxon Valdez Cultural Resource Program*, Mobely, Haggarty, et al, 1990) is useful in understanding the makeup of intertidal areas in the park. When the tide is low, these varied layers of life stripe the steep walls of the fjords like a multicolored bathtub ring.

Supralittoral Fringe Zone This is the highest zone and is sometimes called the "splash zone." The organisms here are nearly terrestrial. They are rarely, if ever, submerged, but they enjoy the constant misting of ocean spray. This zone shows as a diffuse, dark band and includes species of *Porphyra* algae and the black encrusting lichen *Verrucaria maura*. The small, drab colored periwinkles *Littorina sitkana* patiently glide through this zone, scraping the algae and lichen from the rocks.

Littoral Zone The littoral zone encompasses the entire area from mean high water to mean low water, that is, the whole area that fluctuates regularly from total submersion to exposure. It is often separated into subzones.

> Subzone A: The Barnacle Zone As the name implies, this subzone is dominated by several species of barnacles, those jagged little crustaceans that firmly glue themselves to rocks, pilings, boat bottoms, and even whales. They feed by waving their feathery legs through the water to direct food down into their shells. You will find *Littorina sitkana* again, scraping its

way around alongside various *Collisella* limpets. You will also see tufts of the red alga *Endocladia muricata* here.

Subzone B: The Fucus Zone   This subzone is characterized by the brown alga *Fucus distichus,* or rockweed. At the ends of its branches there are often swollen air sacs that pop like little balloons when stepped on. In protected waters, rockweed can form dense canopies, hiding everything else in this zone from view. Brushing back the luxuriant brown growth, though, will reveal snails, barnacles and crowded beds of blue mussels, the most abundant bivalve in the Kenai Fjords intertidal zone. The snails are carnivorous members of the genus *Nucella* and are important predators of barnacles, drilling tiny holes in their outer shells and injecting a toxin before devouring the soft inner flesh.

Subzone C: The Rhodymenia Zone   This is a zone of red and green algae, the dominant species sometimes being *Rhodymenia palmata*. In Kenai Fjords, certain alga species of the genus *Palmaria* are often more common than *Rhodymenia*. Creatures include the algae grazing chitons *Katharina tunicata* and the predatory sea stars *Pisaster ochraceus* and *Evasterias troschelii*. They feed on mussels and other bivalves and may wander into higher zones on rising tides.

Subzone D: The Alaria Zone   This zone is characterized by several species of long bladed brown kelps of the genus *Alaria*. You will also find chitons, sea urchins and sponges here, as well as the large, many-legged sunflower stars *Pycnopodia helianthoides*.

Sublittoral Fringe Zone   The lowest intertidal zone is almost always underwater, even at low tide, and is dominated by several species of the large brown kelp *Laminaria*. There may also be species of gritty, coralline algae present here, along with the limpet *Acmaea mitra* and some of the more mobile creatures from the upper zones.

There are many more species in the intertidal zone—far too many to mention them all. This rich blend of plants and animals provides habitat for small fish, crabs and octopus, and provides a feeding ground for larger animals such as sea otters and shore birds. This blending of two worlds, the gradual edge between land and sea, is perhaps the most complex and least understood environment in all of Kenai Fjords.

The Coastal Forest

Just beyond the busy sea lies a world of cool, muffled stillness. Thick evergreens poke their ragged branches skyward, shading the earth below. The quiet is broken only occasionally by the chatter of a red squirrel or the sigh of an ocean wind in the trees. In contrast to the raw power of the sea, the forest seems a gentle, protected place, the edges softened by clumps of thick moss.

The initial sense of silence slowly gives way, though, and the forest takes on a calm life of its own. Chickadees chatter overhead, and ferns wave gently in the breezes. The flute-like calls of the hermit thrush rise from nearby alder thickets. Tiny red-backed voles scamper across rotting logs and swift sharp-shinned hawks dodge through the trees. A black bear may wander by in search of ripening berries.

The evergreen forests of Kenai Fjords consist primarily of Sitka spruce, mountain hemlock and western hemlock. Nourished by the frequent rains, these trees may live for 700-800 years and form open, park-like stands with an understory of blueberries, salmonberries, devil's club, ferns, and mosses. An easy way to tell the trees apart is by the bark; the spruce has grey, scaly bark while the hemlock's is deeply furrowed. If the trees are young and short enough, just feel the needles. If they poke you hard it's a spruce. Hemlock needles are soft and flat with rounded ends. The berries growing beneath these trees provide food for a number of forest dwellers, including song sparrows, voles, and black bears. With the exception of the Exit Glacier area and the western portion of Nuka Bay, brown bears are absent from Kenai Fjords.

These lush forests are interrupted here and there by other plant communities. Occasional bogs and ponds harbor skunk cabbage, bog orchids, water lilies, and dragonflies. The trees sometimes rise from the ocean edge, but in other places they are fronted by cobble beaches and meadows of beach pea, goose tongue, rye grass, fireweed and lupine. Brushy stream courses provide habitat for river otters, mergansers, and mink. The "edge effect" of these adjacent habitats enhances the diversity of life in the fjords.

The coastal forest is limited to a discontinuous, narrow band extending from sea level to around 1,000 feet above sea level. The elevation of the upper tree line varies considerably based on localized weather and terrain features. For example, in upper Aialik Bay the frequent cloudiness and steep, shady walls combine with all the floating ice and the proximity of the Harding Icefield to keep temperatures too cool for spruce to germinate. Though this area has been ice-free for hundreds of years, there is no evergreen forest at all. Many of the steep walls are also swept so frequently by winter avalanches that they are kept clean

Moose are abscent from most of the park coastline but are common in the Exit Glacier area. / NATIONAL PARK SERVICE

of large trees. These areas are covered instead by dense, nearly impenetrable thickets of low growing, supple Sitka alder. With rising elevation, average temperatures drop and eventually the climate is too cold for the forests. The spruce and hemlock give way in many places to a narrow band of alder, which fades quickly into the low, open alpine community.

Alpine Tundra

It is a cold world, a world swept by wind and buried for months under a heavy blanket of snow. But during the brief respite of the Alaskan summer, it comes alive with a blend of tiny, tenacious plants and hardy animals.

The alpine tundra in Kenai Fjords National Park extends from approximately 1,000 feet above sea level to the tops of the nunataks at over 5,000 feet. Though it is difficult to imagine any area in Kenai Fjords being called dry, the well drained, rocky soils and the near-constant wind of the alpine zone combine to keep it drier than other habitats. Many plants growing here use

The cold, dry winds of the high country desiccate the buds of the trees on the windward side producing the flaglike trees known as "krummholz." / Ed Bovy

Mountain goats are common on the steep upper slopes of the fjords.

long tap roots to reach for water and to anchor themselves against the wind, while others spread their roots widely to insure a foothold. Most grow low to the ground, some forming tight mats or cushions that resemble mosses. This low profile provides a number of advantages: it reduces wind damage to the plant, it allows the plant to take advantage of heat reflecting from the earth, and the tight mats often catch blowing leaves, grass, and soil, providing added nutrients for plant growth. Nearly all alpine plants are perennials which means that they do not have to use an inordinate amount of energy producing flowers and seeds each year, and can, in fact, skip producing seeds altogether in a particularly short or cold summer.

Within the alpine zone, you will find variations in the plant community resulting from variations in soil composition, drainage patterns, and differing "micro-climates." A rocky, well-drained south-facing slope may be sparsely covered with lichens, mosses and a few cushion plants. A moist, gentle slope may be covered with an uninterrupted carpet of mountain heather. A gurgling rivulet may support a lush growth of grasses, sedges and wildflowers along its miniature banks. A wind blasted nu-

PLANT SUCCESSION AT EXIT GLACIER

As glaciers recede, they open up wide expanses of unvegetated land—often bare bedrock or near-sterile plains of rocky debris. The transformation of this land from barren to forested proceeds in stages, with certain plant communities dominating for awhile, only to be taken over by other plant communities until a mature forest finally develops. This process is known as plant succession and it occurs in one form or another not only where glaciers recede, but anywhere where a major event has laid the land bare, such as by fire or flooding.

Among the earliest colonizers in the Exit Glacier area are fireweed, black cottonwood and feltleaf willow. The root systems of these plants develop a mutually beneficial, or "symbiotic," relationship with fungi known as *mycorrhizae* that helps them absorb nutrients more readily from the poor soils. The seeds of these plants and the spores of the fungi are carried into the area by the wind. It is unclear just how or when the plants make contact with the fungi, but without it they would probably not survive. On smooth bedrock surfaces, lichens are the first colonizers, slowly breaking down the rock surface and aiding in soil development. The constant shifting and flooding of Exit Creek often wipes out many of these early colonizers, and re-colonization and re-flooding may continue for 30 or 40 years before stream banks and ground surfaces are stabilized.

Once the ground is stabilized, the colonizers will begin to mature and enrich the soil with leaf litter and other debris. They are joined by other plants and soon green patches dot the rocky plain. These patches are made up primarily of young black cottonwood, feltleaf willow and the fast-growing Sitka alder. These mixed patches will expand and grow, dominating the area for about 40 years.

The black cottonwoods eventually grow taller than the brushy alders and willows, shading them out and taking over. Mature cottonwood forests with an understory of bluejoint grass and scattered spruce seedlings are next in the line of succession, dominating for a hundred years or so. As the cottonwoods grow taller and the soil is further enriched, Sitka spruce, a species that thrives even in the shade, begins to grow up beneath it.

A mixed forest of old cottonwoods and maturing spruce occupies the area for the next 50 years or so until the spruce finally outgrow the cottonwoods and shade them out. Hemlock trees sprout and mature beneath the spruce and the forest eventually develops an open understory of mosses, ferns and berries. This spruce-hemlock forest, sometimes called the "climax community," will prevail until the glacier advances again, wiping the slate clean for the next round of plant succession.

Plant succession is taking place not only in the Exit Glacier area, but wherever fresh land has been revealed by receding glaciers in the park. It is particularly apparent near the Pederson Glacier, the glaciers of Northwestern Fjord and throughout the upper end of McCarty Fjord.

natak may be nearly bare on one side, while its protected lee may be speckled with dwarf wildflowers. As with any natural ecosystem, our descriptions are merely guiding generalities—the real thing is a great mosaic of specifics resulting from hundreds of special circumstances and changing variables.

In the lower alpine areas, well-watered benches and protected depressions may be dominated by heathers, such as Aleutian mountain heather (*Phyllodoce aleutica*) or Alaska moss-heath (*Cassiope stelleriana*). These are low growing evergreen shrubs that often form continuous mats. They have needle like leaves and clusters of small, bell-shaped flowers at the ends of their branches. You may also find a variety of wildflowers reaching skyward at the edges of these evergreen mats, including Nootka lupine, narcissus-flowered anemone, forget-me-not and wild geranium.

Higher alpine communities contain a wide variety of grasses and sedges of the families Poaceae and Cyperaceae. Their thin-bladed profiles and simple flower structures make them well adapted to this windy world. They also are a favorite food of the mountain goats.

Hundreds of these sure-footed beasts roam the mountains of Kenai Fjords, the nannies and kids in bands of a dozen or more, the billies often alone. They move through some of steepest, most treacherous terrain inhabited by any large mammal with a deliberate gait of cool confidence. You may see them occasionally at seaside satisfying their taste for salt, but summer usually finds them fattening-up in the high country. By late fall, the males and females come together for a brief mating period. The billies scratch at the ground, roll in the dirt and clash horns in preparation for the females. They flick their tongues wildly at a receptive nannie and arouse her by kicking her in the rump. After mating, the goats may linger in the alpine into the winter, scratching away the snow to reach their feed, but most often the deep snowcover will force them down to treeline, where they may spend hours or even days lying still, occasionally reaching up to feed on hemlock boughs. The pregnant nannies carry a developing kid inside through the winter months, giving birth in late May or early June. By then the alpine zone is being freed from its winter snows and the goats are ready to fill their bellies on succulent grasses once again.

The grasses, berries, mosses and lichens of the high country provide food for another furry mountain creature, the hoary marmot. These large cousins of the squirrel are more often heard than seen. Their high pitched warning whistles echo throughout the Kenai Fjords valleys all summer long. Their mottled fur and their talent for remaining motionless make them difficult to spot among the lichen-speckled rocks. A keen observer, though, may see one sunning itself atop a boulder on the way up the Harding Icefield trail. They've even been spotted on occasion from kayaks, scavenging along the coastal beaches.

Another well-hidden but common dweller of the alpine zone is the ptarmigan. All three ptarmigan species, the willow, rock and white-tailed, are found in Kenai Fjords, and all three generally spend summer above treeline. They produce a variety of strange cackles, gargles, croaks and whistles, and can often be approached quite closely. Their mottled brown, black and grey plumage disguises them well in summertime. During winter, they turn nearly pure white and can hide in an open field of snow. Other birds of the alpine zone include rosy finches, water pipits and snow buntings.

A dragonfly atop the Harding Icefield reminds us that life can exist under extreme conditions. / Bud Rice

Unegkurmiut mask
COURTESY PAT WILLIAMS/PHOTO BY JIM PFEIFFENBERGER

CHAPTER 3

The People Left Behind
and the People Who Stayed

THEY PADDLED THESE NARROW BAYS and inlets long before anyone called them "fjords." They built homes on the rugged shores.
Their lives were driven by the seasonal cycles of abundance and
want. They gathered roots and berries, they fished, and they
hunted. The Unegkurmiut, or "people over there," were a maritime people, living on the land but oriented toward the sea, draw-
ing their sustenance from the waters around them. They developed a unique material culture of stone and bone tools and were
skilled woodworkers. They were expert boatbuilders and mariners, plying the tempestuous Gulf of Alaska in open skin boats
called *angiaqs* and wood-frame kayaks. Though the fjords are
essentially uninhabited today, the Unegkurmiut, a Pacific Eskimo people, once called them home.

The archaeological record of Kenai Fjords National Park is
incomplete at best. The local geology has not been kind to the
remains of ancient cultures. Seismic activity continually drops
the coastline and old coastal village sites could lie well underwater today. The pulse of glacial advance and retreat has also
done its part to obliterate potential remains, wiping the slate

clean in some areas as recently as 100 years ago. The culture that once existed in these fjords may remain forever shrouded in mystery. Some clues have persisted, though, and archaeological research in the park continues to shed more light on the human history of this rugged coastline.

The southern coast of the Kenai Peninsula was occupied by a distinct group of Pacific Eskimos known as the Unegkurmiut. They are considered close relatives of the Koniag people of Kodiak Island and the Alaska Peninsula, and of the Chugach people of Prince William Sound. These three groups—the Koniag, Chugach, and Unegkurmiut—are collectively known as the Alutiiq people. The Alutiiq shared a common language which differed only in dialect and also shared many cultural traits. In fact, the little that is known about Unegkurmiut culture is actually inferred from studies of Koniag and Chugach cultures. Even the name we have for them, *Unegkurmiut*, is a Chugach word, variously translated as "the people left behind," "the people way out there," or "the people over there."

These were maritime people who took to the sea to provide for themselves. They hunted sea otters, sea lions, harbor seals and whales from their kayaks beginning in early spring and continuing through the following fall. They harpooned their prey with barbed spear tips made of bone that detached from their wooden shafts on impact. The tip, connected by sinew line to an inflated sealskin float, slowed the flight of wounded prey. They hunted whales with slate-tipped harpoons dipped in a poison derived from the local monkshood plant. They also visited bird rookeries in spring to collect both the birds and their eggs. Through the summer they fished for herring, halibut and cod.

By late summer, streams were filled with salmon and the people set up temporary camps nearby to harvest the bounty. The annual return of the salmon was the single most important event for their survival. They laid up large stores of smoked and dried fish against the harsh winter. In late summer and early fall, some hunted mountain goats while others gathered berries.

JIM PFEIFFENBERGER

Projectile points serve as a reminder of the people who lived in the Kenai Fjords area for thousands of years.

Winter was the time of social ceremonies and village life. Their homes were shallow pits lined with wood and covered with roofs of logs and sod. They burned whale and seal oil in decorated stone lamps to light the long nights. Food stored through the summer was supplemented with shellfish and kelp, and elaborate feasts and rituals were performed. The cycle began anew each spring with the return of milder weather and seasonally abundant species.

Very few sites in Kenai Fjords National Park have been excavated, and the oldest known artifacts date to around 700 AD. These artifacts are not particularly old, considering that items dating back to more than 4000 BC have been found on nearby Kodiak Island. Recent work in Aialik and Harris bays suggests that some sites may have been occupied as recently as 100 or so years ago. A census of Alaska conducted in 1880 reported 32 people living in the village of Yalik in the southern portion of the park, but they relocated soon after to the villages of English Bay (now known as Nanwalek) and Port Graham on the western side of the Kenai Peninsula.

Although the constant geological disturbance of the fjords accounts in part for the lack of archaeological remains, another explanation is that the Kenai Fjords coastline may have been only sparsely inhabited all along. Though the area seems abun-

ALUTIIQ CULTURAL CHRONOLOGY
(adapted from *The 1989 Exxon Valdez Cultural Resource Program,*
Mobley, Haggarty, et. al)

Ocean Bay I Period: 5000 BC - 2500 BC
Though the south Alaska coast may have been settled as early as 7000 BC, the first evidence of a truly maritime culture appears during this period. Coastal peoples hunted and processed whales, seals, sea otters and sea birds with chipped stone tools.

Ocean Bay II Period: 2500 BC - 1500 BC
This period is marked by a transition to a new technology of ground slate tools.

Kachemak Period: 1500 BC - 1000 AD
A long period of settlement and population growth. People gathered together in large villages and the first pit houses appeared. They decorated their tools and made pottery. This period is also marked by increasing social complexity; communities evolved into stratified societies of elite, commoners, and slaves.

Late Prehistoric Period: 1000 AD - 1741 AD
The technologies and cultural distinctions which the first European explorers encountered were refined during this period. The Alutiiq peoples developed large stone splitting adzes with wooden hafts for falling trees and woodworking. They fashioned beautiful wooden masks and staged elaborate ceremonial feasts. They decorated their tools and weapons with the likenesses of birds and marine mammals. They trapped salmon with ingenious wooden weirs. When the Europeans arrived, they found a rich, proud culture on the southern Alaska coasts.

JIM PFEIFFENBERGER

CULTURALLY MODIFIED TREES

Culturally modified trees, or "CMTs," are one of the more conspicuous clues from the Native past that remain along the Kenai Fjords coastline. Native dwellers often stripped large pieces of bark from the sides of spruce and hemlock trees, leaving scars we can still see today. The typical scar is a foot or two wide, square at the bottom and tapered at the top. The bark was used for roofing pit houses, as a quick and simple basket or plate, and possibly other unknown purposes. The scars also provided sticky pitch for waterproofing the seams of skin kayaks. Some archaeologists speculate that scars were intentionally maintained on all landing beaches so that kayakers could make easy repairs anywhere in the fjords.

dantly rich to us today, resources are relatively poor when compared with those of Kodiak Island, Cook Inlet or Prince William Sound. The salmon runs are small. The surrounding terrain is difficult for hunting and prone to frequent avalanching in winter. Protected landing sites are scarce—an important consideration for people who travel almost exclusively by boat. Though people certainly did inhabit this area, there are indications that some of the known sites may have been temporary seasonal camps rather than year-round villages. Many more years of research are necessary for a clearer understanding of Unegkurmiut culture to emerge. Until then, the aboriginal dwellers of Kenai Fjords National Park will remain shrouded, like a dark spruce forest wrapped in fog, in mystery.

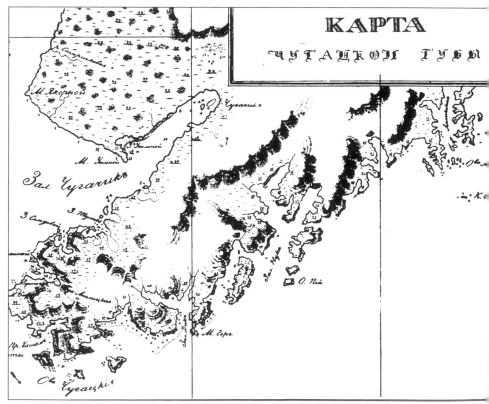

An early Russian map of the southern coast of the Kenai Peninsula. From Teben'kov, approximately 1849.

Construction of the Phoenix in Resurrection Bay by the Russians in 1794.
ANCHORAGE MUSEUM OF HISTORY AND ART

The Russian Period

After weeks of sailing treacherous, uncharted waters, Captain Commander Vitus Bering and his men saw the clouds part one day to reveal a frightening chaos of snow-covered peaks. The year was 1741, and they were the first Europeans to sight Alaska. Bering did not linger in this rugged, wild place, and though his contact with the Native peoples was brief and uneventful, it marked the beginning of major changes in the way of life for the Alutiiq people. Other Europeans soon followed, including the Spanish captain Lopez de Haro in 1788 and the English captains James Cook in 1778 and George Vancouver in 1794. Most influential, though, were the Russians, who came and stayed. They established a colony on Kodiak Island in 1784 and soon expanded into Cook Inlet and Prince William Sound. Their goal was to supply the Chinese market with sea otter pelts. Their method was to coerce Native hunters to do the hunting in kayaks while they supervised. They brought with them trade goods, liquor, Christianity, firearms and disease.

The toll on Alaska Natives was heavy during the hundred or so years of Russian colonialism. Populations were decimated by smallpox and venereal diseases. The traditional way of life was disrupted. Instead of hunting various sea mammals and fish for subsistence, most adult males were forced to hunt only the sea otter from April through September, often hundreds of miles away from their home villages. Huge, Russian-led fleets of Native kayakers were sometimes beset by ocean gales or besieged by fearsome Tlingit Indians, and scores of men were often lost in a single storm or attack. An estimated 11,000 or more Alutiiq people lived along the southern coast of Alaska when the Russians first arrived. By the time they left, fewer than 2,000 Alutiiq remained.

There is little mention of the Kenai Fjords National Park coastline during the Russian period. The English Captain Vancouver wrote in 1794 that "we could not avoid remarking, that the whole of this exterior coast seemed to wear a much more wintry aspect than the countries bordering on the more northern inland waters [Cook Inlet] we had so recently quitted." The Russian Captain Teben'kov published an atlas in 1852 in which he described the park's coastline as being "mountainous, steep and rocky, covered with forests; the gorges and eroded mountains are in many places covered with glaciers....It has....severity of climate, wildness of nature and inaccessible bottom [for anchoring]." Though accurate charts and descriptions of the area apparently existed as early as 1786, the inhospitable nature of the Kenai Fjords led most early mariners to steer well clear.

The Russians likely pursued sea otters into the fjords on occasion, and there is even some evidence that a trading post may have existed in Aialik Bay. The only well documented Russian activity in the park's vicinity was the settlement in Resurrection Bay. In 1793, under the leadership of Alexander Baranov, a small fort and shipyard were established somewhere near the present location of Seward. The exact site remains a mystery.

What is known is that Baranov and his men endured months of cruel hardship and hunger in their little fort while building the 73-foot *Phoenix*. They relied heavily on local Native allies for food and supplies, and in the fall of 1794, the first ship built in Alaskan waters was launched in Resurrection Bay. The *Phoenix* served in Russian America for five years before sinking somewhere in the stormy North Pacific.

By 1867, the Russians had seriously depleted the sea otter stocks and were having difficulty financing further exploration in their far-flung colony. Then U. S. Secretary of State William Henry Seward negotiated for the purchase of the territory for 7.2 million dollars, or about two cents per acre. Though many in Congress opposed the purchase, "Seward's Folly" turned out to be quite a bargain indeed.

The Seward wharf leading into Fourth Avenue, 1906.
RESURRECTION BAY HISTORICAL SOCIETY

The American Period

The Yankee traders who took control in the late 19th century showed even less restraint than their Russian predecessors. They pursued the struggling sea otter into its last refuges and mercilessly slaughtered it along with other furbearers. They traded guns and whiskey to the Natives and completed the coastal culture's transition from a subsistence lifestyle to a cash economy.

The Alaska Commercial Company was at the center of this fur industry. They maintained a trading post at English Bay and had a substation at Yalik for collecting furs taken in the Nuka Bay area. The presence of this post may account for the 32 people recorded living on the park's coastline in 1880. The pursuit of the sea otter was so reckless, though, that by 1910 just 29 pelts were taken in all of Alaska. International treaty finally put an end to the slaughter in 1911. By that time, the remaining Unegkurmiut of the Kenai Peninsula coastline, dependent

Two pioneers of the park's coastline, Mr. and Mrs. "Herring Pete" Sather. Herring Pete had a fox farm on Nuka Island and a gold claim on the nearby mainland.

ANCHORAGE MUSEUM OF HISTORY AND ART/B91.46.105, PHOTO BY JEANNE SCHAUER BOONE TAKEN IN 1952

now on a cash economy, had all but abandoned their traditional homeland in favor of the fish canneries of Port Graham and Seldovia.

It wasn't long, though, until another fur craze swept the Kenai coast—not sea mammals this time, but foxes. In 1920, fox pelts brought up to $120 apiece. The strategy was simple—find an island, set some foxes loose, then trap them as needed at baited feeding stations. Fox farms were established on the Chugach Islands at the southern tip of the peninsula, on Fox Island in Resurrection Bay and on Nuka Island near the park's southern boundary. The foxes were fed on salmon and herring seined from local waters, and the "farmers" resorted to such tactics as shooting bald eagles and cutting down their nest trees to minimize the loss of valuable fox pups. Though the market for fox pelts crashed in the early 1930s "Herring" Pete Sather and his wife Josephine maintained their fox farm on Nuka Island from 1921 until 1961, when Herring Pete disappeared at sea in a storm while en route to Seward.

Along with the fox farmers, there was another breed of hardy souls scratching out a living in the Nuka Bay area in the early 20th century—hard rock miners. They staked their claims in the difficult terrain around West Arm and Beauty Bay as early as 1909. In 1918, someone finally struck gold. Though not the richest paydirt on the Kenai Peninsula, persistent mining from the 1920s through the 1940s pulled more than $150,000 worth of gold from these remote lode mines, a quantity worth more than $2.5 million at today's prices. The mines bore such colorful names as "Paystreak" and "Golden Goose," and hopeful miners dug more than a thousand feet of tunnel into the Sonny Fox mine. Some of the easiest profits, though, may have been realized by "Smokehouse" Mike and George Hogg who, rather than mining, devoted their efforts to running a liquor still during the early days of prospecting. Mining efforts were renewed in the 1960s with some success and today there are still three active claims within the park. Under current federal regulations, no new claims can be filed within the park, but visitors are free to keep whatever gold they might pan by hand.

The early 1940s saw a great flurry of activity in Alaska as the U.S. rushed to defend its northern territory from Japanese invasion. The Aleutian Islands were attacked in 1942, and there was fear that the mainland could be next. The port of Seward was considered particularly strategic since it provided the connection between ships and rail lines to the interior. Fortifications were hastily built in Resurrection Bay and the population of Seward mushroomed. Though no fighting ever ocurred here, there were unconfirmed reports of enemy periscopes spotted near the entrance to Resurrection Bay. Signs of the wartime activity still persist in and around Seward in the form of the Army Recreation Camp, the many quonset huts around town and the fort ruins at Caines Head State Recreation Area.

During the 1950s and 1960s, the fjords saw some use by commercial fishermen, shrimpers and bounty hunters. The State of Alaska offered bounties on harbor seals at this time; they were considered a threat to the fishing industry. The waters near the heads of the fjords were easy seal-hunting grounds since the seals liked to haul out and rest on the icebergs there. One story has it that a bounty hunter working in Aialik Bay shot so many seals one summer that he broke the territorial bank when he turned in his skins.

Establishment of the Park

With the passage of the Alaska Statehood Act in 1958, the State of Alaska was given the right to claim title to more than 100 million acres of land. Though the protection of lands traditionally used by Natives had been promised for years by the federal government, virtually no land had ever been officially granted to any Native group. It soon became clear that State claims to land conflicted with Native claims of traditional use.

The issue of who had rights to which land remained unresolved through the 1960s. Finally, spurred by desires for further oil development in Alaska, Congress passed the Alaska Native Claims Settlement Act (ANCSA) in 1971. Signed into law by President Nixon on December 18 of that year, ANCSA confirmed title to 40 million acres of land for Native groups and also gave them more than 900 million dollars as compensation for lands lost.

Another provision of ANCSA allowed for the creation of new national park, national forest and national wildlife refuge units as well as the expansion of existing units. In 1978 President Carter created the 567,000 acre Kenai Fjords National Monument by presidential proclamation and in 1980 the area was designated a national park with the passage of the Alaska National Interest Lands Conservation Act (ANILCA). Though the spectacular, wild beauty of the Kenai Fjords had always been known to the local residents, it was now recognized and protected by the whole nation. Visitors have been flocking to the park in increasing numbers ever since and the stunning scenery is now world-renowned.

Though national park designation typically protects an area from major development or private ownership, the Kenai Fjords case is unique. The descendants of the Unegkurmiut people living in Port Graham and Nanwalek are entitled to land claims under ANCSA. Since all of the land in the immediate vicinity of their villages is already owned or claimed by someone else, they were given selection rights within Kenai Fjords National Park. Currently, about 70,000 acres of coastal land in the park have been selected by the villages and conveyances began in 1995. Check with the park for any changes in backcountry use regulations resulting from these transfers. Efforts are underway by the federal government to purchase any of the selected lands that the Native villages are willing to sell. This would bring them permanently under the protection of the National Park Service.

The Oil Spill

Midnight, March 24th, 1989 was a fateful hour for Kenai Fjords National Park. More than 100 miles to the northeast, tanker Captain Joseph Hazlewood went below deck and left third mate Gregory Cousins in charge of piloting the *Exxon Valdez*. The rest, as they say, is history. When the *Exxon Valdez* first began leaking oil into Prince William Sound, there was little concern about the distant Kenai Fjords. Despite reassurances from Exxon and Coast Guard officials that no oil would leave the sound, cleanup efforts floundered, and on April 10, 1989, Kenai Fjords National Park was fouled by the largest oil spill in U.S. history.

Some 12 miles of the park's coastline were eventually oiled to some degree. On its way to the park, the oil passed directly through the Chiswell Islands, where it wiped out thousands of seabirds. Seals, otters, and eagles were also killed by the oil, as well as untold numbers of smaller organisms in the intertidal zone. Most heavily hit were areas in the southern portion of the park, including Taroka Arm, McArthur Pass, Beauty Bay, Black Bay and Yalik Bay.

Cleanup crews worked the beaches in the park during the summers of 1989 and 1990. Some methods used in other areas affected by the spill, such as hot water washing, were considered too intrusive by park officials. The hot water virtually sterilizes the intertidal zone, killing the organisms adapted to cold-water. The National Park Service favored less detrimental methods such as cold water washing and careful removal of oil with hand tools. It was impossible to remove every last trace of oil using these methods so nature was left to finish the job. Visitors won't readily see oil in the park today, but careful observation might still reveal disintegrating globs and patches tucked away on rocky beaches.

The most notable ongoing impact of the oil spill is the disruption of bird breeding cycles. The two species most obviously affected are the common murre and the harlequin duck. As of 1994, both species still appeared to be experiencing high rates of reproductive failure in the Kenai Fjords area. The precise cause for the failure is unknown, but could be the result of ongoing habitat degradation caused by the presence of oil in the ecosystem. Researcher are concerned about other bird and animal species, too, such as black oystercatchers and sea otters.

Perhaps one of the only benefits of the spill was that scores of previously undocumented sites were discovered by survey crews working throughout Prince William Sound and the Kenai Peninsula coastline. Never before had so many people systematically walked every beach in these remote areas. Though the archaeological information gathered is certainly valuable to our understanding of the pre-history of the Kenai Fjords, the price for its discovery was high. The full impact of the *Exxon Valdez* oil spill may never be known, but it was clearly harmful and will, we hope, never be repeated.

BLM

Oil containment booms stockpiled at the Port of Seward.

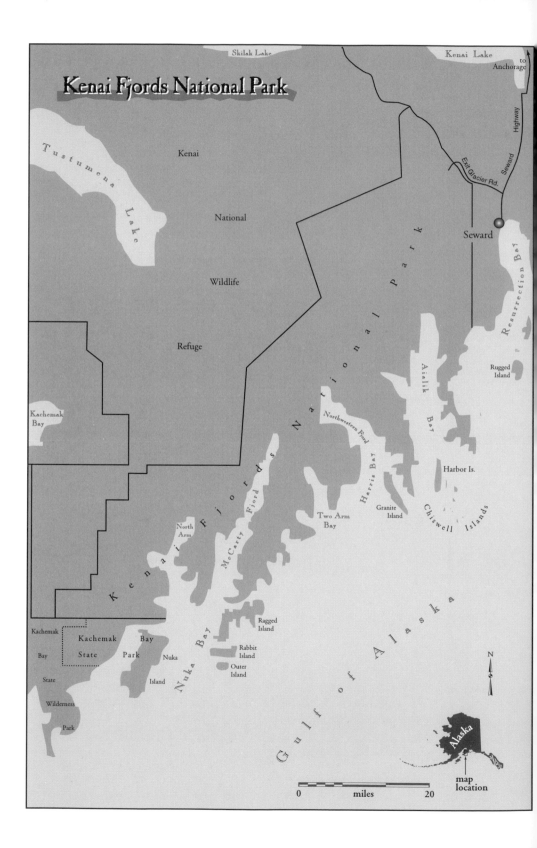

CHAPTER 4

Exploring Kenai Fjords

Tour Boats

THE SIMPLEST WAY TO EXPERIENCE the beauty of Kenai Fjords is to take one of the all day boat tours that leave from Seward during the summer months. Several private companies offer such tours; check with the Kenai Fjords National Park visitor center or the Seward Chamber of Commerce for current schedules.

These tours start in Resurrection Bay and typically cruise south along the coast toward Aialik Cape. At Caines Head, you'll likely encounter your first puffins of the trip. If you miss them here, though, not to worry—there are plenty more ahead! You'll pass the beautifully curving Bear Glacier, longest of the more than 35 glaciers that spill from the Harding Icefield. Look for the dark stripe of rocks, or medial moraine, that runs down its center, indicating where separate tributary flows of ice come together. In addition to the mountain scenery, you may also see bears and mountain goats on the towering slopes and sea otters, porpoises and whales in the surrounding waters.

Aialik Cape is where the best scenery really begins. Huge granite slabs, part of the Harding Icefield batholith, maintain a foothold at the edge of the Gulf of Alaska, where they are pounded by winter storms and washed by summer tides. Bald eagles nest atop this majestic cape and horned puffins find homes in its fractured walls. Once around the cape, you enter Aialik Bay, a wild, rugged place where glaciers meet the sea.

Most of the tours will visit Three Hole Point, a rocky headland where rain, wind and waves have combined to create a set of natural arches, and then continue on to Holgate Arm. An underwater sill, or old glacial moraine, marks the entrance to Holgate Arm. Though you won't see the sill itself, you may see evidence of it in the form of seabirds, sea lions or even humpback whales diving and feeding in this area. The shallow sills tend to harbor rich concentrations of marine life.

As you continue up Holgate Arm, the temperature will drop rapidly as you approach Holgate Glacier. Be sure to bring plenty of warm clothes so that you can stay out on deck and watch the glacier calve icebergs into the sea. Listen for loud pops and creaks from the splintered ice. If you listen carefully, you'll even hear the icebergs around the boat snapping and crackling as they melt and tiny bubbles of compressed air are released. And if you happen to be looking in the right place at the right time,

CLOTHING SUGGESTIONS FOR BOAT TOURS

Dress as you would for a cold winter ski trip: long johns, heavy gloves or mittens, warm wool or pile layers covered with a wind and waterproof outer shell, and a warm hat. You can always peel this stuff off if it happens to be an unusually warm day, but you'll be mighty glad to have it when the wind is coming down off the glaciers. The speed of the boat will accentuate the natural sea breeze, and without several warm layers, you'll be inside instead of out on the front deck enjoying the best views of the wildlife and scenery. A broad-brimmed rain hat is also recommended. If you're really lucky, you'll end up using it to shade your face from the blinding sunlight reflecting off the glaciers! Also don't forget to throw in some high energy snacks to help keep you warm from the inside and plenty of extra film for your camera.

EDWARD BOVY

Tour boats, both large and small, venture to the glaciers daily in summer.

you'll see chunks of ice break free of the glacier to become icebergs. This spectacular phenomenon of tons of ice collapsing
and crashing into the frigid ocean, known as *calving*, is an experience never to be forgotten.

Besides being an awesome sight, the calving of the ice also
helps provide food for the local seabirds. Look for flocks of kittiwakes and gulls swarming near the face of the glacier where
an iceberg has just crashed into the sea. The turbulence resulting from the falling ice stirs up a rich broth of tiny shrimp and
other organisms that help sustain these seabirds. It is easy to
lose your sense of scale in the presence of a massive tidewater
glacier—the birds flying near its face can help give you some
sense of how close or far you are from the ice.

Your tour will likely continue on to the Chiswell Islands,
part of the Alaska Maritime National Wildlife Refuge, to see
the prolific seabird rookeries there. The isolation of these steep
granite islands provides excellent protection from predators, and
seabirds flock here by the tens of thousands each spring to breed

and raise their young. Raucous clouds of black-legged kittiwakes spin near the cliffs, and horned and tufted puffins inter-
mingle on the water. Common murres crowd the ledges, and
you may also be lucky enough to spot thick-billed murres, red-
faced cormorants or parakeet auklets. The Chiswells are also a
favorite haulout for Steller sea lions and a great area to look for
whales, bald eagles and peregrine falcons.

As you cruise back toward Seward, on a clear day you'll see
the brilliant white blanket of the Harding Icefield stretching high
and flat across the top of the Kenai Mountains. The tour boats
typically cruise further offshore on the way home, which provides a good opportunity to look for pelagic birds such as sooty
shearwaters, fork-tailed storm petrels and northern fulmars.

For those with less time to explore, some of the tour companies also offer half-day tours in Resurrection Bay. Though you
won't see a tidewater glacier actively calving icebergs into the
sea, you will still see some fantastic scenery, including the hanging glaciers of Thumb Cove and the sinuous lines of the massive
Bear Glacier. Marine life in Resurrection Bay is abundant, and
chances of seeing puffins, sea otters, sea lions, porpoises and
whales are excellent.

Cruising the Fjords

Those with private boats can explore the park more at their
leisure and have the opportunity to see seldom visited areas such
as Harris Bay, Paguna Arm, Thunder Bay and the Nuka Bay
area. Bear in mind that storms are frequent and can be fierce at
any time of year. Anchorage can be found in the following locations (from north to south) along the park's coastline:

Bulldog Cove: Protected from weather out of the south.
Beware of williwas, or strong, unpredictable winds, coming out
of the north off Bear Glacier. Not well protected from southeast
or north winds.

Agnes Cove: Good mud bottom in the southeast corner. Protected from all directions.

Paradise Cove, Three Hole Bay: Though popular with some mariners, Paradise Cove is subject to williwaws due to the low, narrow passes on each side.

Coleman Bay: The south bight provides protection in all kinds of weather. Probably the best anchorage in Aialik Bay.

McMullen Cove: Good protection. Watch for shoals extending westward from the beach.

Verdant Cove: Good protection during the milder summer months. Either tuck in close near the south point rock, or go all the way to the south end.

Taz Basin, Granite Island: Narrow entrance with rock in the middle opens up into a beautiful, calm embayment. Good protection in most weather.

Crater Bay: Excellent protection in the southernmost bight.

Otter Cove, Northwestern Lagoon: First cove on the west side just inside the glacial moraine that marks the entrance to Northwestern Lagoon. It's a favorite spot with sea otters. Use caution entering the lagoon as the moraine is hidden at high tide but extremely shallow. Enter just 50 - 150 yards from the eastern shore, then swing back to west to the cove. There are many rocks in the middle of this cove. Use caution and keep to the northwest side.

Taroka Arm: The lagoon in the western corner offers excellent protection, but is shallow. Beware of minus tides.

Thunder Bay: Good bottom and excellent protection in the northeast corner.

Black Bay: The northwest side of the northernmost bight offers fair protection, but is exposed to south and southeast winds.

McArthur Cove: Mud bottom in the south end. This is the best spot in the McArthur Pass area.

Desire Creek area: Good bottom with protection from the south on the north side of the spit, but exposed to north wind.

Yalik Bay: All the way back against the northwest side affords some protection.

Alaska State Ferry

The Alaska State Ferry system connects Seward with Homer, Kodiak Island, Unalaska and Prince William Sound. Check with the Alaska Marine Highway office in Seward or call 1-800-642-0066 for schedule information. Walk-on spots are easy to come by, but if you are planning to take a vehicle on the ferry, you should make reservations well in advance. It's a very pleasant and relaxing way to let someone else do the driving while you soak up the scenery. Though the ferry generally stays well offshore, there are good opportunities to view seabirds, whales, and other marine life from the deck. On runs between Kodiak and Seward, you may see the flat white expanse of the Harding Icefield stretching across the upper reaches of the Kenai Mountains. And be sure not to get stuck below decks when rounding Cape Resurrection on the way to or from Prince William Sound—the boat passes near the prolific bird rookeries of Barwell Island, a sight not to be missed!

A kayaker is dwarfed by Pederson Glacier. / Jim Pfeiffenberger

Kayaking the Fjords

Travelling by sea-kayak is the most ideal way to experience the park's coastline. You can linger or travel as you please, and get a feel for how the earliest human inhabitants saw this area. You can pull up and wander the beaches, or drift among icebergs and rocky islands studded with sea stars and mussels. You can observe seals, sea otters and whales at relatively close range, and you can feel the power of the ocean surging beneath you. Sea-kayaking in Kenai Fjords is a quiet, intimate, unforgettable experience.

Though there are a few coves that are protected and calm in virtually any weather, the Kenai Fjords in general are exposed to the whims of the Gulf of Alaska and are not waters for beginners or inexperienced paddlers. The power of the ocean is always close at hand here. Landings can often involve some surf, particularly when afternoon breezes kick up from the south. Wind and rainfall can be excessive, and summer storms often push an ocean swell of three feet or more into the fjords. Though weeks of calm may sometimes persist during the summer, stormy conditions can strike any time of year. Paddlers with less experience may wish to travel with one of the many licensed guide services that operate in the park. Check with the park headquarters in Seward for a current list of guides.

Paddling directly from Seward is fine for day trips in Resurrection Bay or overnight visits to Caines Head or even Bear Glacier, but it is not recommended for those wishing to explore Aialik Bay or points further south. There are long stretches of exposed coastline with no landing sites between Callisto Head and Aialik Cape, and waters at the cape can be treacherous. Most kayakers choose to access the park by charter boat, leaving from Seward and getting dropped off somewhere in Aialik Bay or Northwestern Lagoon. Kayaking in the fjords is becoming increasingly popular, so don't expect to have the place to yourself. Another alternative is to fly in to the less visited Nuka Bay area

Minimum Impact Camping
in the Marine Environment

Set up camp on bare ground whenever possible rather than trampling beach vegetation.

Keep food out of your camp—it attracts bears and other wildlife. You should cook and stow all food at least 100 yards from your camp. Cook below high tide line when possible; the incoming tide will erase the food smells.

Hang your food from trees, at least ten feet up and six feet from the tree trunk. Many recently deglaciated valleys are treeless; if you plan to camp in treeless areas, bring bearproof food cannisters along for food storage. Failure to properly store your food is punishable by fine and could result in injury to some subsequent camper by habituating wildlife to human food.

Dispose of human waste below high tide line where the cleansing action of the ocean can take effect. This can be achieved by either doing your duty below high tide line, or, if the tide is in, depositing waste on a large, flat rock, then tossing it into the sea. In protected coves with little wave action, deposit human waste six inches below the soil surface and at least 100 yards from fresh water sources. Pack out or burn your toilet paper.

Use camp stoves instead of fires. Driftwood fires are usually smoky and smelly anyway, and they leave the beach littered with unsightly charred logs. If you must have a fire, build it below high tide line where the ocean will eventually remove its remains.

Be aware of shorebirds, terns and gulls that may be nesting on rocky beaches. A noisy, disturbed, aggressive bird is a sure sign of a nearby nest—do not linger or set up camp in the area; you may step on the eggs or cause them to go cold while the adult bird spends its time trying to chase you away instead of incubating.

Though you may consider your driftwood lounge chair a masterpiece of ingenuity, others will find it an unsightly reminder that this wilderness has been invaded by humans. Break up all driftwood "furniture," tent rings, and fire rings before leaving so that others may find the beach as pristine and "untouched" as you did.

A Few Tips for Kayaking in Kenai Fjords

The waters of Kenai Fjords are only marginally protected and are not for the inexperienced. If you are a beginner, your best bet is to contact one of the licensed guide services and travel with an experienced guide. Call the Park Visitor Center at (907) 224-3175 for a current list of licensed guides.

Bring along an extra tarp or two for securing dry camp space during the frequent prolonged periods of rain. A good sense of humor also helps weather these storms!

Once the rain stops, the bugs come out! Bring headnets and light gloves for hand and wrist protection. Insects can be fierce in the fjords.

Never approach a tidewater glacier any nearer than half a mile distant, and stay in deep water where waves from calving ice will not break, but will simply pass under you as a swell.

Do not land anywhere within two miles of a tidewater glacier. Waves from calving ice can slam the shore with surprising power and kayaks and gear stowed well above the apparent tideline can be swept away.

Be aware that most of an iceberg is hidden below the waterline and they regularly shift and roll. Do not approach them too closely.

Use caution when entering Northwestern Lagoon, James Lagoon or McCarty Lagoon. Tidal currents can create standing waves, boils and confusing eddies. It is best to enter these lagoons at high, slack tide.

Pederson Lagoon should only be entered at high, slack tide. Approach the mouth of the lagoon from the east, not the south, as there is a submerged bar that causes breaking waves immediately south of the entrance. Be sure to sit well offshore and analyze the conditions for several minutes before paddling in.

Use clues such as driftwood accumulation, beach steepness and cobble size to judge what wave action is like in storm conditions. Will you be able to launch from this beach in the morning if the wind or weather changes overnight?

Be prepared to wait out storms for two or three days. There is no reason to get home on schedule that justifies paddling through potentially deadly seas. When in doubt, stay on the beach.

Bring a weather radio along so that you can stay apprised of changing conditions.

What to Wear When Kayaking

Good rain gear is a must. Most "breathable" fabrics are not adequate for the steady, heavy rains on Alaska's coastline. Instead, rubber coated or urethane coated non-breathable fabrics are recommended for the best rain protection. A wide brimmed rain hat is also preferable to a hood while paddling—your vision, hearing and movement are much less obstructed. Waterproof poagies are recommended to keep hands dry and warm.

No matter what the weather, you should always be dressed in warm layers while paddling and prepared for a possible capsize. A neoprene wet suit or waterproof dry suit will greatly reduce the debilitating effects of cold water immersion on your body. Carry a roomy four season mountaineering tent—you may be holed up in it for days and it may be exposed to extreme winds. A spare tarp or two will help you secure more dry living space in the event of an extended storm.

Kayakers should also bring mosquito head nets and light weight gloves for bug protection. The insects can be maddeningly fierce and even the strongest bug dope is no substitute for a good headnet. Be sure to consult books specifically on sea-kayaking for a complete equipment checklist before heading out.

from Homer. Again, check with the Kenai Fjords Visitor Center for information on sea and air charters.

However you get there, you are in for a treat once you're underway by kayak. The peaceful rhythm of dipping your paddle into the cold, deep water is both soothing and refreshing. The surrounding scenery is stunning and almost dreamlike; a favorite activity not to be missed is floating near a tidewater glacier and watching it calve icebergs into the fjord. Be careful, though, not to approach too closely; calving ice has been known to generate huge waves and kayakers in the park have capsized as a result (see "A Few Tips For Kayaking In Kenai Fjords," p. 82). Witnessing these spectacular glaciers at work is an awe-inspiring experience, but remember that their scale and power have no regard for puny human activities.

There are relatively few beaches that are suitable for camping, so you may find yourself sharing your camp with other kayakers. The fact that the same beaches are used over and over again means that the potential for human impact and degradation is great. Please be a good camper and use minimum impact camping techniques.

Public Use Cabins

There are five public use cabins in Kenai Fjords National Park available for a nominal fee. One of them is in the Exit Glacier area and is available for use only during the winter months when snow closes the road (approximately December to March). The other four are in remote areas along the park's coastline and are available for use during the summer months only, from May to September. These cabins are in high demand, so reservations must be made well ahead of time. You can make reservations by calling the park headquarters in Seward at (907) 224-3175, or by writing to:

Kenai Fjords National Park
P.O. Box 1727
Seward, Alaska 99664

Reservations for the summer season are not accepted until January 1. Reservations for the winter season are accepted beginning on October 1. When staying in the public use cabins, please remember that you are still in a wilderness setting full of wild animals—all food should be stored inside and doors and windows closed when you leave the cabin to explore.

Exit Glacier Public Use Cabin: There is a public use cabin at Exit Glacier that is available only during the winter months. Access is by ski, snow machine, dogsled or snowshoes. The cabin sleeps four comfortably and comes supplied with propane heat and cooking facilities. Exact dates of availability will vary from year to year depending on snow. Ski and snow machine trails in the Exit Glacier area are maintained by park rangers.

Aialik Bay Public Use Cabin: Built in 1985, this is the oldest public use cabin in the park. It is located on the east side of upper Aialik Bay, just north of Coleman Bay, and is marked by an triangular orange trail sign at the edge of the brush. The cabin sleeps just three or four comfortably, but there is room to set up a tent out front under a big spruce tree. The landing here is rocky—it is best to land a bit north of the orange cabin trail marker, then walk down the beach to the trail. There is a beautiful lagoon behind the cabin that is frequented by mergansers, river otters and black bears. Pink salmon spawn in this lagoon in late August and early September. They can sometimes be caught from the beach beginning in late July. Fresh water can usually be found running from the cliffs north of the cabin. This cabin also has a wheelchair ramp connecting the front porch with the outhouse.

Holgate Arm Public Use Cabin: This cabin was built in 1991 and features a fantastic view of Holgate Glacier right out the front door. This cabin will sleep six or more people comfortably. The thundering rumble of a good-sized glacier calving will rattle the windows! The trail leading up the beach to this cabin is 50 yards or so east of the cabin itself. Do not attempt to climb the steep bluff directly below the cabin as it is hazardous and contributes to the erosion of the bluff. Fresh water can sometimes be found near the trail to the beach but by late July it is a good idea to bring extra water with you. This cabin is surrounded by an enormous blueberry patch—good eating in August, but watch for bears! Another thing to keep in mind is that Holgate Arm is popular with tour boats. From around 11:30 a.m. until 2:30 p.m. you are likely to share this lovely fjord with the sight and sound of power boats, but evenings will be all yours.

Delight Spit Public Use Cabin: This cabin sleeps six to eight comfortably and is located near the park's best fishing spot. There is a light run of red salmon up Delight Creek during July, and a good run of silver salmon in August, heaviest in late August. There are good-sized Dolly Vardens here, too. Alaska state fishing regulations apply in all waters within and surrounding the park. Headnets and hand protection are a must; insects can be fierce here all summer.

North Arm: This cabin also sleeps six to eight comfortably. Landing here can be problematic due to shallow tide flats. At low tides you may be more than 100 yards from the beachfront. Headnets and hand protection are a must; insects can be fierce here all summer.

Camping at Exit Glacier

The National Park Service maintains a primitive campground located near Exit Glacier. There are eleven walk-in tent sites, a water pump and outhouses. Camping is free but there is a fourteen day limit. Four fire pits near the parking lot serve as cooking areas. Do not cook in the tent sites since both brown and black bears frequent this area. Store food in vehicles or hang it from the line near the outhouses. There are no facilities for RVs in the Exit Glacier area and overnight parking is not allowed in the Exit Glacier parking lot.

Exit Glacier Trail / Edward Bovy

Hiking Trails

The only developed trail system in the park is in the Exit Glacier area. A bulletin board near the parking lot describes current trail conditions. There is also a ranger station with maps and interpretive information. Short, ranger-guided hikes are usually offered during the summer months; these are a wonderful opportunity to learn about the Exit Glacier area more in-depth. Check at the park visitor center in Seward for exact times.

A paved, wheelchair accessible trail leads from the parking lot out to a covered shelter with a fantastic view of the glacier. From here, a gravel trail leads to the open outwash plain in front of the glacier. Here you can see kettle ponds, glacial moraines and the deep blue crevasses of Exit Glacier at close range. Be careful, though, not to go beyond the posted warning signs or attempt to walk on the ice—the glacier is active and chunks of ice weighing tons can fall at any time!

Once you're done gasping at the glacier's granduer, take a look around at the patches of moss, dwarf fireweed and even spindly, stunted cottonwoods—life returning in the wake of the ice. The dwarf fireweed is particularly beautiful from mid-July through mid-August. You may also encounter birds like American dippers, semi-palmated plovers or violet-green swallows while exploring the outwash plain. Moose and black-bears sometimes wander in to view here, too. Remember, they are wild animals. Do not approach them intentionally! The steep slopes to the north are home to a band of mountain goats that often spend summer days grazing in high, open meadows; bring along a pair of binoculars to watch them.

A short, steep trail winds up to a beautiful overlook on the bedrock hills just north of the glacier. Be sure to look for glacial striations, or scratches, in the rock and listen for pops and groans coming from the ice. Also look for the trim lines on the valley walls that mark Exit Glacier's former extent.

A nice alternative for returning to your car is to take the

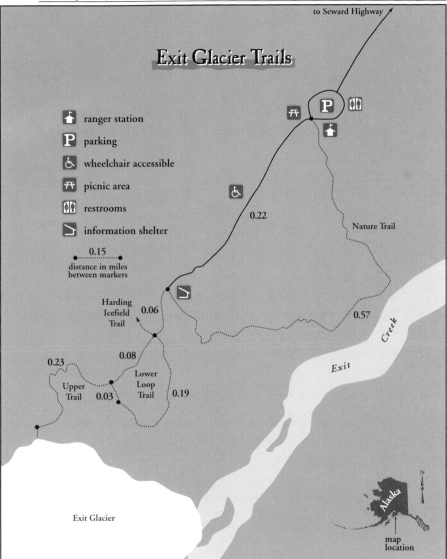

Exit Glacier Trails

- 🛈 ranger station
- 🅿 parking
- ♿ wheelchair accessible
- ⛢ picnic area
- 🚻 restrooms
- ⛴ information shelter

• 0.15 •
distance in miles
between markers

to Seward Highway

Nature Trail

0.22

0.06

Harding
Icefield
Trail

0.08

0.23

Upper
Trail   0.03

Lower
Loop
Trail   0.19

0.57

Exit   Creek

Exit Glacier

N

Alaska

map
location

nature trail which splits off at the end of the paved trail and
winds back to the parking lot through a young forest of alder,
willow and cottonwood. A series of signs along the way inter-
prets the plant succession that follows glacial recession. Look
for wildflowers here: lupine, pink pyrola, and yellow dryas in
the early summer, sidebells pyrola and fireweed among others
later. Note: Pets are prohibited on all Exit Glacier trails.

Harding Icefield Trail: This 3.5-mile-long trail begins 50 yards or so beyond the end of the paved trail and offers one of the most spectacular views available on foot in Southcentral Alaska. The trail was originally established by mountaineers as a route for accessing the icefield, and it is a steep and strenuous hike. Those with the time and energy to tackle it, though, will be rewarded with outstanding views of Exit Glacier, the Resurrection River valley and the Harding Icefield. You may also see bears, mountain goats, marmots and natural gardens of fragrant wildflowers along the way. Ranger-guided hikes up this trail are usually offered on summer weekends. Check at the park visitor center for an exact schedule.

The Harding Icefield Trail corridor is designated by the National Park Service as a day-use area only; any overnight camping must be done at least 1/2-mile from the trail and only on snow or bare, unvegetated rock. Alpine tundra vegetation is extremely fragile so watch where you step! There is a small day-use shelter at the end of the trail where hikers can seek temporary refuge from wind and weather. Be aware that the upper reaches of this trail may be snow covered until well into July, and use of an ice axe may be advisable. Dress warmly, plan on spending all day to get up and back, and be sure to sign the register at the trailhead before hiking. Note: Pets are prohibited on the Harding Icefield Trail.

Hiking the park's rugged coastline is a more ambitious undertaking. There are no developed trails and access is by boat or plane only. Though there are some beautiful expanses of alpine tundra and high hidden lakes, getting to them often requires hours of difficult bushwhacking through alder thickets. Alpine areas are typically snow-covered until mid July. On the other hand, beaches and recently de-glaciated valleys are relatively open and provide ample opportunity for exploration. Anyone wishing to hike on the park's coast should have good map-reading and route-finding skills, and should also be prepared to encounter extended periods of heavy rain as well as bears and other wildlife. Guns are allowed in all areas of the park for protection from wildlife, but hunting on park lands is illegal.

Mountaineering

The Harding Icefield offers excellent mountaineering possibilities. Parties wishing to explore the icefield should be well-versed in glacier travel and crevasse rescue techniques and should ideally be experienced skiers. People also can travel on the icefield with snowshoes. The icefield is most easily accessed via Exit Glacier on the east side and via Tustemena or Chernof glaciers on the west side. Storms sweep in from the Gulf of Alaska quickly and regularly and can bring winds in excess of

Mountaineers set up camp atop the Harding Icefield. Snow walls protect their tents from the ever present winds. / SUSAN PFEIFFENBERGER

100 miles per hour with them. Anyone attempting to travel on or traverse the icefield should be prepared to be pinned down by wind and whiteout for days at a time. Travelers should also rope together whenever moving on the icefield as buried crevasses can be encountered anywhere. Successful traverses of the icefield have taken anywhere from six days to two weeks, and many parties have been turned back by the weather. Those lucky enough to have good weather, though, can experience an awesome glimpse back into the ice age, when entire continents were dominated by glaciers. Isolated nunataks jut up from the vast white expanse like dark islands in a smooth sea, begging to be explored. The view from the summit of one of these granite peaks is indescribably beautiful and eerie.

Winter Activities

During winter, a relative calm falls over the park. The chattering of the thousands of seabirds is replaced by the sigh of a steady north wind. Black bears, fat from gorging on fall berries, retire for their long winter's sleep. Streams once splashing with salmon lie frozen and still. First the high country, then the forests and even the beaches are buried by heavy snows. As storm after storm sweeps in off the Gulf of Alaska, the glaciers are replenished against their summer losses. Boats are infrequent visitors to the fjords this time of year. The silence is more likely to be broken only by the rumble of a distant avalanche or the crash of a wind-driven wave.

Exit Glacier is the only part of the park that sees much human activity during the long winter months. When the road and vast outwash plain in front of the glacier are buried under snow, they become ideal for skiing, dog mushing, and riding snowmachines. Park rangers are on duty year-round at the glacier and, conditions permitting, they groom the snow into a network of trails that allow easy access to the quiet winter scenery. This is the best time of year to look for moose at Exit

Glacier. Their big, dark, hulking bodies are easy to spot with the leaves gone and the background white. A public use cabins is available for overnight stays during winter (see p. 84). There is nothing quite like skiing past a moonlit glacier with the northern lights flickering overhead and a warm cabin waiting just minutes away!

Weather

The weather is both boon and bane of the Kenai coast. Without the frequent storms, there would be no snow, no Harding Icefield, no Exit Glacier and no deeply-carved, spectacular fjords. The storms that help create this beauty, though, often preclude enjoying it. Many have suffered through rough seas and wind-driven rain in hopes of spotting a whale or watching a glacier calve icebergs. Many others, though, have had the luck of clear skies and calm seas and have witnessed the fjords revealed in all their beauty. Still others like best watching the veils of mist swirl and wrap around the forested slopes. What this adds up to is that you can expect heavy, cold rains at any time of year, and that cloudy, cool weather is more common than sunshine. Each summer is different, but in general June is the driest month, with precipitation increasing throughout the summer. The following tips and weather data gathered at Exit Glacier may shed some light on what to expect. Keep in mind that Exit Glacier is slightly warmer and dryer than the coastal fjords.

EXIT GLACIER WEATHER

Month	Avg . High	Avg. Low	Avg. Precip.
May	55 F	32 F	3.8 inches
June	64 F	39 F	1.9 inches
July	66 F	44 F	3.7 inches
August	63 F	42 F	9.0 inches
September	55 F	34 F	11.4 inches

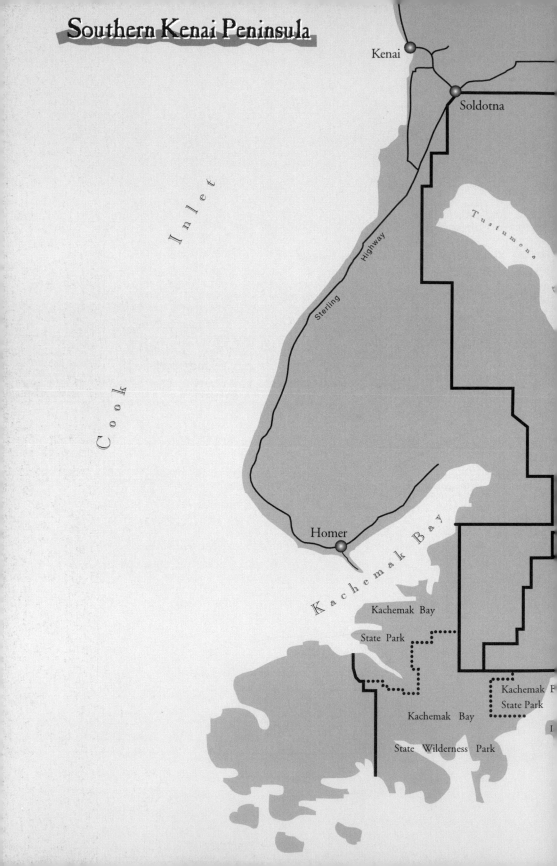

Southern Kenai Peninsula

Kenai

Soldotna

Cook

Inlet

Tustumena

Sterling

Highway

Homer

Kachemak Bay

Kachemak Bay
State Park

Kachemak Bay
State Park

Kachemak Bay

State Wilderness Park

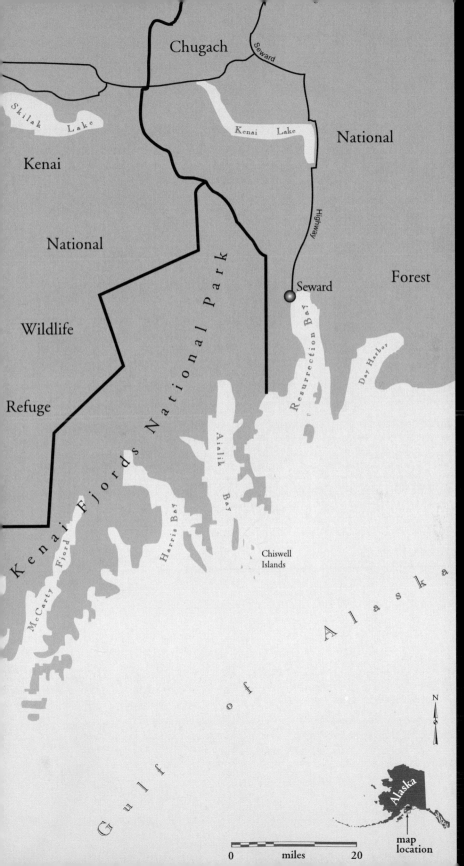

Chugach

Seward

Kenai

Skilak Lake

Kenai Lake

National

National

Forest

Wildlife

Seward

Refuge

Resurrection Bay

Day Harbor

Kenai Fjords National Park

Aialik Bay

Harris Bay

Chiswell
Islands

McCarty Fiord

Gulf of Alaska

N

map
location

Alaska

0   miles   20

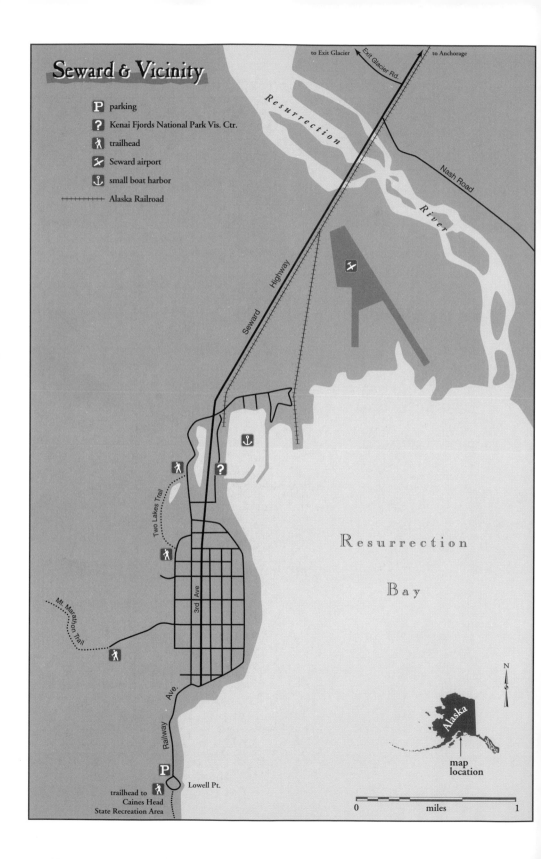

Seward & Vicinity

P   parking

?   Kenai Fjords National Park Vis. Ctr.

🚶   trailhead

✈   Seward airport

⚓   small boat harbor

++++++++++   Alaska Railroad

to Exit Glacier

Exit Glacier Rd.

to Anchorage

Resurrection

Nash Road

River

Seward Highway

Two Lakes Trail

Mt. Marathon Trail

3rd Ave

Railway Ave.

Resurrection

Bay

N

Alaska

map
location

P

trailhead to
Caines Head
State Recreation Area

Lowell Pt.

0   miles   1

CHAPTER 5

Seward

Seward lies nestled between steep, jagged mountains at the head of Resurrection Bay. The glacially-shaped peaks and narrow bay make a dramatic backdrop for this small community, one of Alaska's oldest. Though not part of Kenai Fjords National Park, Resurrection Bay is a glacier-carved fjord, nearly a thousand feet deep. The depth of the bay helps keeps it ice-free year round, a major reason for the founding of Seward here in the first place.

Around the turn of the century, a few hardy Americans were busy discovering the mineral wealth of Alaska. Gold, copper and coal were all known to exist in commercially viable quantities by 1900. Resurrection Bay was already in use as a steamer port at this time, though there was no real town nor any port facilities to speak of. In 1902, though, a survey party arrived searching for a good starting point for a rail line to the interior. The timbered flatland at the head of this deep, ice-free bay was just what they were looking for. On August 28, 1903, Captain E. E. Caine brought the steamer *Santa Ana* into Resurrection Bay and dropped off 83 men, women and children, along with provisions and construction supplies to begin work on the Alaska

Central Railroad. Their goal was to build a rail connection to the coal fields of interior Alaska.

Completing the rail line proved to be a slow-going process fraught with both logistical and financial difficulties. The town became a busy port and a popular jumping-off spot for prospectors bound for the gold fields of the interior. Particularly active at this time were the gold fields of Nome and the Iditarod River region. In 1908, the Alaska Road Commission surveyed a new trail from Resurrection Bay to Nome, with one branch leading to the Iditarod gold fields. Seward became the official "Mile 0" of the Iditarod Trail, later made famous by the annual sled dog race. Today, a portion of the historic trail serves as a bike path along the Seward waterfront while other parts of the trail just outside of Seward are still popular with dog-mushers and skiers.

RESURRECTION BAY HISTORICAL SOCIETY

Seward has been a gateway to the Alaska interior since the day it was founded. These adventurers are about to set out for the gold fields near the town of Iditarod in interior Alaska.

The young city of Seward went through a quick series of booms and busts as railroad projects started, then failed. Several historic homes belonging to early bankers and railroad barons still stand in Seward, particularly along the crest of the hill on Third Avenue, an area once known as "Millionaire's Row." The continuing failure of private railroad companies finally led the federal government to take over the project in 1914. The rail connection with Anchorage was completed in 1918, and eventually tracks were laid to the interior. Seward grew into a vital shipping link and was the main port for supplies entering Alaska for years.

With the onset of World War II, more than 3,000 soldiers arrived to help guard the strategic port from enemy attack. A flurry of construction activity left Seward with an improved airport and a large fort complex that was eventually converted into today's Army recreation camp. There are also several old army quonset huts around town that now serve as homes, garages and workshops. Ruins of the harbor defenses remain in several locations around Resurrection Bay, including Barwell Island and Caines Head.

Seward's role as port facility for all of Alaska was altered forever one fateful day in just a matter of minutes. The day was March 27, 1964, when the Great Alaska Earthquake struck. Nearly a mile of Seward's waterfront broke free and slid into the bay, taking rail lines and other heavy equipment with it. This underwater landslide displaced thousands of tons of water and sent a huge wave known as a seich wave racing across Resurrection Bay. Upon reaching the other side, the wave sloshed back and headed toward Seward. By this time, a series of leaks and explosions at the waterfront Texaco fuel storage facility had sent a flaming petroleum sheen out into the harbor. It must certainly have seemed like a vision of the Apocalypse when the wave rose up as a flaming wall of water and slammed down on the wrecked town. The tsunami wave came next, lifting and tossing a diesel locomotive some 200 feet like a child's

Seward was one of the communities that suffered greatly from the 1964 earthquake. Many buildings along the waterfront were destroyed by a tsumani, a huge earthquake-generated wave that swept across Resurrection Bay.

toy. In the end, 11 people lost their lives, 86 houses in Seward were completely destroyed and 269 houses were heavily damaged. Road and rail lines were severed, and the industrial port was effectively destroyed. The Great Alaska Earthquake encouraged the opening of shipping lanes in Cook Inlet so that boats could directly access Anchorage. Seward's shipping importance faded, though today there is still an industrial dock used mainly by coal transport ships. A modern marine repair facility exists on the east side of Resurrection Bay. The rise of Alaskan tourism makes Seward an active cruise ship and recreational port during the summer months.

Ironically, the city of Seward was originally opposed to the establishment of Kenai Fjords National Park in 1980 and the city council even passed a proclamation stating as much. Millions of acres of land were taken over by the federal government around this time, and the general feeling among Alaska residents was that the "feds" were locking up the land and taking away Alaskans' rights to use it. The economic advantages of having a national park nearby became quickly apparent as park-loving tourists flocked to Seward. The city council rescinded their proclamation of opposition in 1985, and welcomed Kenai Fjords National Park as a good neighbor.

Things to See in Seward

Kenai Fjords National Park Visitors Center. The Park Visitor Center is located near the small boat harbor at 1212 Fourth Avenue. It features interpretive displays on the fjords, glaciers and the Harding Icefield; an information desk staffed by rangers; and also houses the park's administrative offices. There is a small auditorium where slides and videos are shown and special evening programs are presented by park rangers. Check at the information desk for a schedule of events. Books, videos, posters, postcards and other items related to the park are also available here.

Seward Museum. Located at the corner of Third and Jefferson in the Seward Community Center, the Seward Museum houses an extensive collection of photos from the early railroad days of the town. There are also a wide variety of exhibits, including information on Native arts and crafts, Russian shipbuilding efforts in Resurrection Bay, Rockwell Kent's stay on Fox Island, President Warren G. Harding's visit to Seward, World War II in Alaska, the Great Alaska Earthquake and other events of local interest. Evening programs on the history of Seward and the history of Iditarod Trail are presented regularly. Check at the museum for a schedule of events.

Benny Benson Memorial. Alaska's striking state flag, eight gold stars on a field of blue, was designed by Seward's own Benny Benson in 1927. Benny was an orphan who lived at the Jesse Lee Home for orphans from all over Alaska. He was just 13 years old when his design was chosen to represent the state. The Jesse Lee Home no longer operates, but Benny Benson's contribution to the history of Seward and the whole state of Alaska is commemorated at this memorial at the north end of the lagoon.

Institute Of Marine Sciences, K.M. Rae Building. Located at 125 Third Avenue, the K.M. Rae Building houses exhibits on the marine life of Resurrection Bay and the Gulf of Alaska. There is also a fine auditorium here where films, videos and programs are presented during the summer. Check at the K.M. Rae Building for a schedule of events.

Camping in Seward. The City of Seward maintians three public camping areas. The largest and most popular is along the waterfront just opposite Ballaine Boulevard. Another waterfront site, Spring Creek Camping Area, is located on the east side of Resurrection Bay at the end of Nash Road. This area is popular during the late summer when silver salmon are abun-

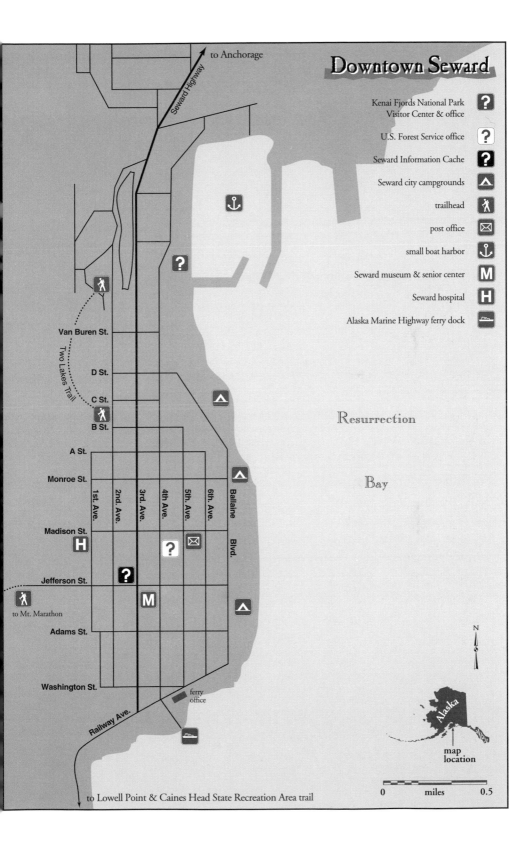

Downtown Seward

Kenai Fjords National Park Visitor Center & office	?
U.S. Forest Service office	?
Seward Information Cache	?
Seward city campgrounds	▲
trailhead	🚶
post office	✉
small boat harbor	⚓
Seward museum & senior center	M
Seward hospital	H
Alaska Marine Highway ferry dock	⛴

to Anchorage

Seward Highway

Van Buren St.

Two Lakes Trail

D St.

C St.

B St.

A St.

Monroe St.

1st Ave.

2nd Ave.

3rd Ave.

4th Ave.

5th Ave.

6th Ave.

Ballaine Blvd.

Madison St.

Jefferson St.

to Mt. Marathon

Adams St.

Washington St.

Railway Ave.

ferry office

Resurrection

Bay

N

Alaska

map location

0   miles   0.5

to Lowell Point & Caines Head State Recreation Area trail

dant. A third camping area is located on Hemlock Street just off the Seward Highway about two miles north of downtown. Tent and RV camping is allowed at all three camping areas, but there are no hook-ups available. A nominal nightly fee is charged. For information on camping at Exit Glacier, see p. 86.

Hiking Trails Near Seward

Two Lakes Trail. This approximately one-mile loop winds past two small lakes through the forested hills just above Seward. Park behind the Alaska Vocational Technical Center buildings on 2nd Avenue or at the end of Vista Street near Second Lake to begin the hike.

Primrose Trail. This thirteen-mile round trip leads to Lost Lake from the north. The trail is steep and moderately strenuous and begins at the Primrose Campground, mile 17.2 of the Seward Highway. Remains of old mining activity can be found along the trail. Weather is unpredictable, and whiteout can occur in any season.

Resurrection River Trail. This trail parallels the Resurrection River for 16 miles on easy terrain, then ties in with the Russian Lakes Trail which continues on to the Sterling Highway near Cooper's Landing. From there, hikers can continue on the Resurrection Pass Trail, completing a 72-mile-long hike from Seward to Hope. The trailhead is at approximately Mile 7 of the Exit Glacier Road, just east of the bridge that crosses the Resurrection River into Kenai Fjords National Park. A Public Use Cabin is located seven miles in from the trailhead. Inquire at the Chugach National Forest Service office [(907) 224-3374] at 334 4th Avenue in Seward about trail conditions and cabin availability.

Caines Head Trail. A 4.5-mile trail leads from Lowell Point to North Beach at Caines Head. See the section on Caines Head (p. 113) for details.

Exit Glacier Trails. A system of short trails leads from the parking lot to scenic views of the glacier. See "Exploring The Park" (p. 86) for details.

Harding Icefield Trail. A steep, 3.5-mile trail leads up out of the Exit Glacier Valley to spectacular overviews of the Harding Icefield and Exit Glacier. See "Exploring The Park" (p. 88) for details.

Special Events in Seward

Fourth of July. Seward has one of the largest Fourth of July celebrations in all Alaska. Thousands of people flock here for the annual parade and street fair. Most famous, though, is the three-mile Mt. Marathon Race, a mad dash to the top of a 3,022-foot mountain and back. This is one of the oldest organized footraces in the United States, dating back to at least 1915.

Hikers enjoy the supurb view of Resurrection Bay atop Mt. Marathon./ BUD RICE

Legend has it that the race was born as early as 1909 when two sourdoughs made a bet in a local bar, wagering whether a man could make the run in less than an hour. Today, both men and women make it in under an hour, and the event has grown to be one the highlights of the Alaskan summer.

Silver Salmon Derby. The Seward Silver Salmon Derby is another long time Alaskan ritual, the first one having been held in 1955. It occurs during the second or third week of each August when silver salmon are returning to Resurrection Bay in large numbers to spawn. There are cash prizes given to anglers holding derby tickets for the largest and smallest fish caught each day and the largest catch of the whole derby. There are also a few fish released each year with tags worth thousands of dollars to a lucky angler. Contact the Seward Chamber of Commerce at (907) 224-8051 for details on prizes, rules, and prices of derby tickets.

Seward Halibut Derby. Held each summer during the month of July. Contact the Chamber of Commerce at (907) 224-8051 for details.

MARIA GILLETT

EDWARD BOVY

(top) A Polar Bear Jump in January raises money for charity (above) The Chamber of Commerce Information Center is an old 80-foot Pullman parlor car that served the Alaska Railroad in the 1930s..

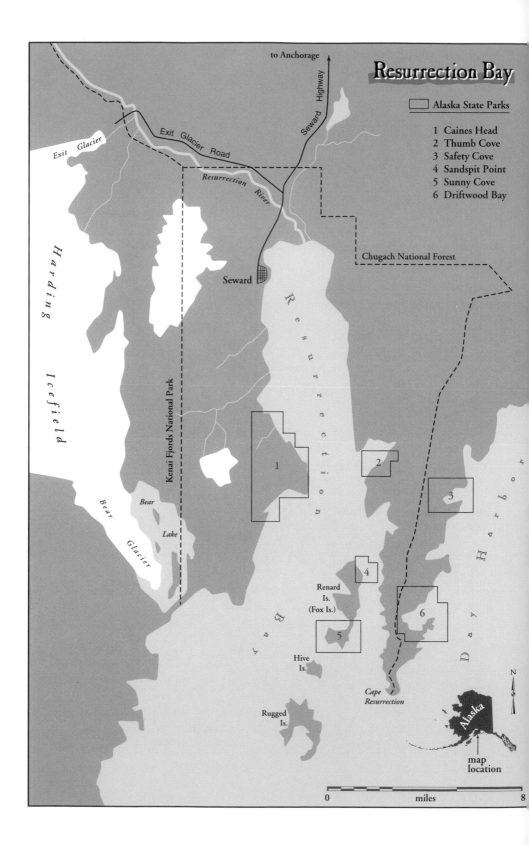

Resurrection Bay

Alaska State Parks

1 Caines Head
2 Thumb Cove
3 Safety Cove
4 Sandspit Point
5 Sunny Cove
6 Driftwood Bay

to Anchorage

Seward Highway

Exit Glacier

Exit Glacier Road

Resurrection River

Chugach National Forest

Harding Icefield

Seward

Resurrection

Kenai Fjords National Park

Bear Glacier

Bear Lake

1

2

3

4

Renard Is. (Fox Is.)

6

5

Bay

Day Harbor

Hive Is.

Cape Resurrection

Rugged Is.

N

Alaska

map location

0   miles   8

CHAPTER 6

Resurrection Bay: Marine Playground

Alaska State Marine Parks

THE STATE OF ALASKA maintains five small state marine parks in the Resurrection Bay area. These are locations that are protected for their scenic and recreational qualities and are also considered good anchorages. The state marine parks include water and tidelands, beaches and some uplands. All five sites are managed and patrolled by the Caines Head rangers.

Thumb Cove This is possibly the best anchorage in all of Resurrection Bay and is well protected from the prevailing south-southeast summer weather. There are also good opportunities for kayak landing and onshore camping. You may see whales, porpoises, sea otters or sea lions in Thumb Cove, and you will find abundant blueberries ripening onshore in the late summer. Though there are currently no developed trails, a little bush-whacking provides access to the rocky alpine zone. Spectacular hanging glaciers cling to the steep walls which rise above Thumb Cove, making it one of the most scenic spots in Resurrection Bay. The State of Alaska is considering plans to improve campsites here and possibly build a public use cabin. Check with state park offices in Kenai (907-262-5581) or Anchorage (907-762-2617) for the latest information.

Sandspit Point and **Sunny Cove** are both located on Fox Island. The island takes its name from the fox farming that occurred here in the early part of the century. Fox Island is also known as the place where artist and writer Rockwell Kent spent the winter of 1918 living in a small cabin, an experience which led to several paintings and woodcuts of the area and to the publication of his classic book, *Wilderness, A Journal of Quiet Adventure in Alaska.*

Sandspit Point is located on the northeast side of the island on a rocky spit which juts out into Eldorado Narrows. The north side of the spit provides reasonably good short-term anchorage but is subject to slippage and exposed to any north wind. The spit is a good kayak landing and campsite. "Ghost forests" line the shores here, eerie stands of dead trees killed when the Great Alaska Earthquake of 1964 lowered the shoreline and dropped the tree roots into saltwater. A brackish pond occupies the center of the spit—freshwater can be hard to come by here so bring plenty if you plan to camp. Just across the narrows from Sandspit Point are the unique pillow basalt formations of the Resurrection Peninsula. This part of the peninsula is made up of uplifted lavas that originally flowed and hardened beneath the sea. Look for mountain goats clinging to the precipitous heights.

Sunny Cove is on Fox Island's west side and is just south of the cove where Rockwell Kent lived in 1918. This area is primarily a scenic, fair weather anchorage. Beware of northeast winds here or west winds off of Bear Glacier. There is private property on the northern portion of the beach and no good campsite in the state marine park, though it is possible to camp atop the rocky beach berm in a pinch.

Seward's status as a major gateway to Alaska continues as record numbers of cruise ships use its fine harbor. Here an outbound ship passes Thumb Cove State Marine Park. / MARIA GILLETT

Driftwood Bay and **Safety Cove** These are reasonably good anchorages on the east side of the Resurrection Peninsula. Access to the land is difficult here and these bays are exposed to east and southeast weather. These two marine parks are recommended for experienced mariners only.

For further information contact:

Division of Parks and Outdoor Recreation
Kenai Area Office
P.O. Box 1247
Soldotna, Alaska 99669
(907) 262-5581

COURTESY ALASKA STATE PARKS / PHOTO BY JACK TURNBULL

EDWARD BOVY

(top) One of the two six-inch gun emplacements at Caines Head, guarding
Resurrection Bay in 1943. (above) Fifty years later, a nearly-identical view
shows how the concrete and steel are surrendering to the native vegetation.

Caines Head State Recreation Area

In the late 1930s, a climate of impending war clouded the international scene. The U.S., though initially determined to stay out of the conflict, strengthened its defenses, including the distant western outposts of Alaska. The deep, ice-free port of Seward was a vital shipping link with rail lines to the interior, and Fort Raymond was established there to protect it. Additional fortifications were set up near the entrance to Resurrection Bay. The most commanding view of the bay is from a rock promontory seven miles from Seward known as Caines Head, and it was here that the 250th Coast Artillery set up their guard. Some 270 men with four 155mm guns were already stationed there by late 1941 when America was drawn into the war.

On June 3, 1942, less than six months after the surprise attack on Pearl Harbor, the Japanese set their sites to the north and attacked the Aleutian port of Dutch Harbor. Just a few days later, they invaded and occupied Kiska and Attu islands. These attacks set off a flurry of activity in Resurrection Bay. A road was pioneered from the beach to a battery site at the top of Caines Head, some 650 feet above the bay. Two six-inch guns were installed to ward off enemy invasion. A fort was established nearby. The 267th Coast Artillery joined the 250th. Barracks were erected on the south beach of this strategic headland and 500 soldiers were housed there.

In all, the military spent $4,727,000 on fixed defenses for Resurrection Bay, most of it on Fort McGilvray at Caines Head. The fort was 90 percent complete by early 1944, but the Japanese had already been ousted from the Aleutians and their military might was fading fast. Though there were a few unconfirmed reports of enemy submarines in nearby waters, Resurrection Bay was never stage to any combat. In light of the diminishing threat, Fort McGilvray was ordered abandoned on April 7th, 1944. Three years later, the military completely dismantled the fort, leaving only concrete and rusting steel where

Munitions storage for Caines Head artillery

soldiers once kept vigil.

Today, nearly 6,000 acres of Caines Head and the surrounding highlands make up Caines Head State Recreation Area. A 4.5-mile-long trail beginning at the Lowell Point parking lot leads past Tonsina Creek to North Beach. Rotting wooden pilings are all that remains of the Army dock that served as a landing for World War II forces. From North Beach, old Army roads have been converted to trails that lead through the thick spruce forest. The right fork of the trail leads to South Beach where the soldiers were housed. Here you'll see the gutted remains of utility buildings and barracks. The left fork leads up past concrete ammunition magazines to the site of the abandoned fort. Here you can see the round concrete pads where the big guns were once mounted and take in the sweeping views of the bay below. Explore the spooky underground passages and rooms of old Fort McGilvray.

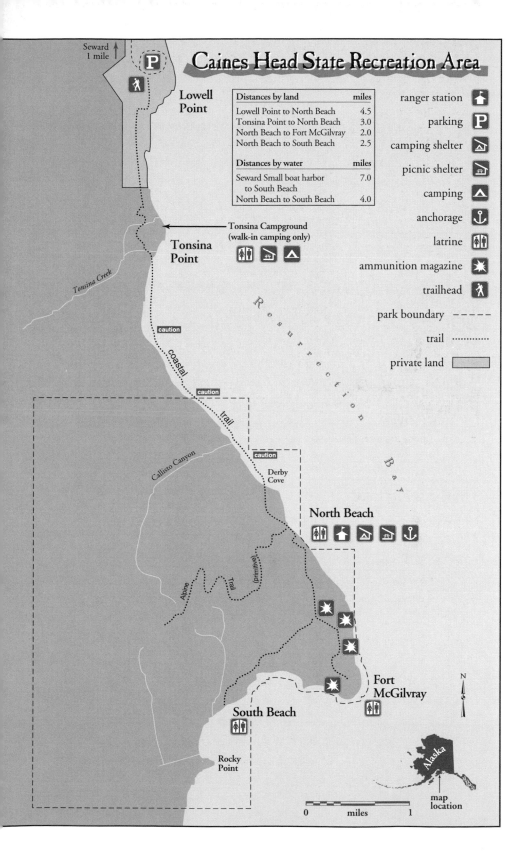

Caines Head State Recreation Area

Seward
1 mile ↑

Lowell Point

Distances by land	miles
Lowell Point to North Beach	4.5
Tonsina Point to North Beach	3.0
North Beach to Fort McGilvray	2.0
North Beach to South Beach	2.5

Distances by water	miles
Seward Small boat harbor to South Beach	7.0
North Beach to South Beach	4.0

ranger station
parking
camping shelter
picnic shelter
camping
anchorage
latrine
ammunition magazine
trailhead
park boundary — — —
trail ·············
private land

Tonsina Creek

Tonsina Campground
(walk-in camping only)

Tonsina Point

Resurrection Bay

caution

coastal

caution

trail

Callisto Canyon

caution

Derby Cove

North Beach

Alpine

Trail

(primitive)

Fort McGilvray

South Beach

Rocky Point

N

Alaska

map location

0   miles   1

In addition to the military ruins, Caines Head also features a taste of the Alaskan natural world. Horned puffins nest on the cliffs here. In fact, this is the closest spot to Seward for seeing these cute, colorful birds. Pigeon guillemots, marbled murrelets, spruce grouse and bald eagles are among the other birds that you'll see in the summer months. Marmots scamper from high country to beach, while mountain goats favor the south-facing cliffs. Black bears roam the woods. The lush spruce forests are interrupted by occasional bog meadows, home to carnivorous sundew plants and delicate orchids. Energetic hikers can scramble up above the trees to open expanse of alpine tundra and bare rock.

The trail from Lowell Point to Tonsina Point is on high, forested ground. There is one camping shelter at Tonsina Point. <u>The trail from Tonsina Point to North Beach can only be hiked at low tide.</u> Check tide tables before attempting this trip.

There are two camping shelters at North Beach, and there is a Public Use Cabin at Derby Cove. The cabin sleeps six and is available year round. It costs $35 dollars per night. Call (907) 262-5581 to make reservations. Campers should remember that bears frequent the Caines Head area. Cook and store food well away from your tent and keep a clean camp.

For further information contact:

Division of Parks and Outdoor Recreation
Kenai Area Office
P.O. Box 1247
Soldotna, Alaska 99669
(907) 262-5581

Alaska Maritime National Wildlife Refuge

The Alaska Maritime National Wildlife Refuge is a sprawling, discontinuous 3.5-million-acre reserve that consists of more than 2,500 islands, headlands, spires, sea stacks and offshore rocks. It stretches from the shores of the Arctic Ocean to nearly the southernmost tip of Southeast Alaska. The refuge was created in 1980 with the passage of the Alaska National Interest Lands Conservation Act to protect critical marine bird and mammal habitat. Eighty percent of the 50 million seabirds which nest in Alaska nest on refuge lands, the bulk of which are located in the Aleutian chain and the Gulf of Alaska.

The main attractions of the refuge in the Kenai Fjords area are Barwell Island and the Chiswell Islands. Barwell Island is located at the tip of the Resurrection Peninsula and is home to thousands of nesting black-legged kittiwakes and common murres every summer.

Boat tours out of Seward sometimes stop here to take in the fascinating, frantic activity of this seabird colony. The Alaska

The isolated islands off the southern coast of Alaska provide critical habitat for marine mammals and seabirds. / National Park Serivce

Marine Highway ferries pass Barwell Island on their way from Seward to Prince William Sound.

The Chiswell Islands are located at the mouth of Aialik Bay and are a highlight of many of the all-day boat tours of Kenai Fjords National Park. Here you will see not only kittwakes and murres, but also horned and tufted puffins, pelagic and red-faced cormorants, parakeet auklets and possibly even a peregrine falcon or two. The steep, offshore granite islands provide the birds good protection from predators, and easy access to fish and other food. In addition to all of the birds, the Chiswells are also a favorite haulout of hundreds of Steller's sea lions.

The Pye Islands and the Barren Islands are also part of the refuge, but are seldom visited by tourists. In fact, no one is allowed to approach the southern tip of the Pye Islands within three miles since there is a major Steller's sea lion rookery there. Steller's sea lions have been steadily declining in number for unknown reasons since the 1970s. The three-mile closure is intended to encourage greater breeding success by allowing the sea lions to raise their young in peace.

The Barren Islands lie just south of the Kenai Peninsula near the entrance to Cook Inlet. The winds and waters of Shelikof Strait, the Gulf of Alaska and Cook Inlet meet here and combine to create frequent fierce storm conditions. This does not seem to bother the seabirds, though. They nest here by the tens of thousands—sooty shearwaters, fork-tailed storm petrels, common murres, marbled murrelets and more. The foul weather only adds to the undisturbed isolation that they love.

Alaska Maritime National Wildlife Headquarters are located in Homer. There is a visitor center at 509 Sterling Highway, Homer (telephone 235-6961) with displays interpreting refuge wildlife and management. Ask here about boat tours on Kachemak Bay to Gull Rock, another part of the refuge that teems with bird life in the summer. Murres, puffins and kittiwakes abound along with occasional red-faced cormorants. Also, keep a sharp lookout for Aleutian terns.

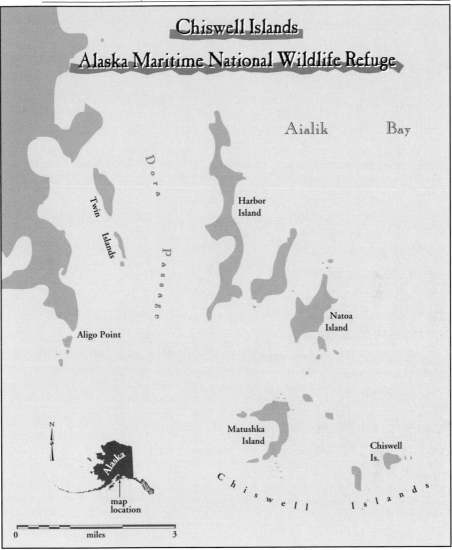

The refuge is managed by the U.S. Fish and Wildlife Service. The protection of these far-flung nesting areas and rookeries helps insure that Alaska's wildlife will thrive for years to come. For further information, contact:

Alaska Maritime National Wildlife Refuge
Box 541
Homer, Alaska 99603
(907) 235-6546

Grewingk Glacier and its origins atop the Kenai Mountains represent a continuation of the Kenai Fjords ecosystem.

CHAPTER 7

Kachemak Bay State Park and Kachemak Bay State Wilderness Park

KACHEMAK BAY STATE PARK, the first legislatively established state park in Alaska, and Kachemak Bay State Wilderness Park, the only legislatively established wilderness in the state park system, occupy nearly 400,000 acres just south and west of Kenai Fjords National Park. Established in 1971 and 1972 respectively, these parks are part of the ecosystmes shared with the nearby national park and national wildlife refuge. Nearly 45,000 acres were added to the state park in 1989, including Nuka Island and most of the uplands and coastline adjoining the national park at Petrof and Yalik glaciers.

Like Kenai Fjords, these parks contain a striking blend of rugged mountains, massive glaciers, rocky beaches and quiet bays. The wildlife found in the forests and surrounding waters includes bald eagles, black bears, moose, mountain goats, whales, sea otters and a wide variety of seabirds and fish. Brown bears are rare in the state park.

Intertidal sealife and many species of birds are found along the shoreline of China Poot Bay, making it popular for bird watching and tidepool exploration. Nearby Gull Island has one of the highest concentrations of nesting seabirds in this part of Alaska and is readily accessible for viewing by tour boats from Homer.

The wilderness park encompasses most of the southern half of the two parks along the Gulf of Alaska. It includes Port Dick, Gore Point and Tonsina Bay. This rugged coastal region faces the open Gulf of Alaska and is seldom visited due to its remoteness and lack of development. The northern part of Kachemak Bay State Park lies within the more protected and sheltered waters of Kachemak Bay. A short boat ride from Homer will bring you to the trail system in and near Halibut Cove Lagoon. Nearly thirty miles of developed trails will lead you to some of the park's most beautiful features. There is a ranger station and a Public Use Cabin and ranger station in the lagoon area.

Sea-kayaking is one of the best ways to explore the coastal beauty of Kachemak Bay. Kayakers should bear in mind, though, that Kachemak Bay tides are among the largest in the world, averaging 15 verticle feet, with an extreme season high of 28 feet. Tide books, available at sporting goods stores, are essential! Use the Seldovia tables. Boaters must use U. S. Coast and Geodetic Survey marine charts to safely navigate the through the fjords, bays and coves of the area.   Be sure your boat is secure before leaving it—the rising tide has been known to carry kayaks away with it! If you are boating for the first time into some of the lagoons and bays, it is recommended to not only have the proper marine charts, but also to talk to a local fisherman or park ranger who has navigated in these waters.

Weather also is a consideration as it can change several times a day. Bring extra food and dry clothing as rough seas can keep you shorebound and add unexpected days to your trip.

Fishing for Dolly Vardens from the beach is generally good all summer. A Fish and Game-enhanced run of king salmon returns to Halibut Cove Lagoon in late May and early June, and red salmon make their way up the creek at the head of China Poot Bay at the end of July. In addition, China Poot lake is stocked

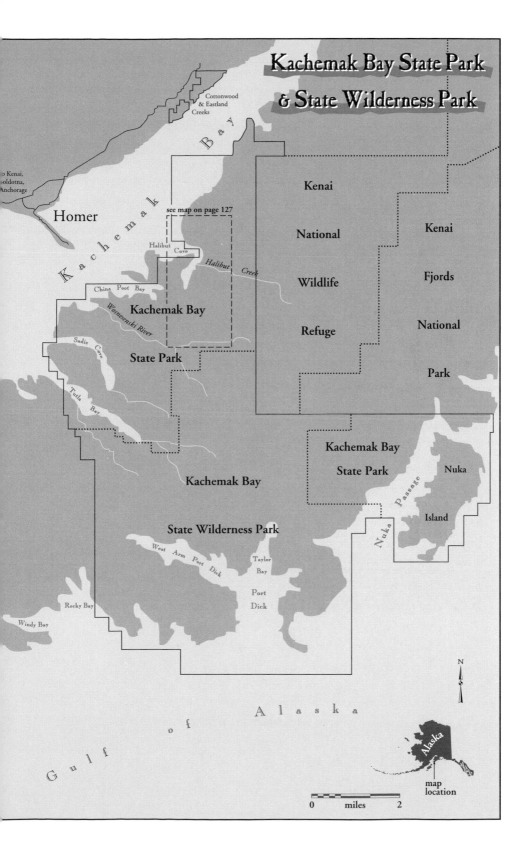

Kachemak Bay State Park
& State Wilderness Park

Cottonwood & Eastland Creeks

Kachemak Bay

to Kenai, Soldotna, Anchorage

Homer

Kachemak

see map on page 127

Kenai

National

Kenai

Halibut Cove

Halibut Creek

Wildlife

Fjords

China Poot Bay

Kachemak Bay

Wosnesenski River

Refuge

National

Sadie Cove

State Park

Park

Tutla Bay

Kachemak Bay

State Park

Kachemak Bay

Kachemak Bay

State Park

Nuka

Nuka Passage

Island

State Wilderness Park

West Arm Port Dick

Taylor Bay

Nuka

Port Dick

Rocky Bay

Windy Bay

N

G u l f   o f   A l a s k a

Alaska

map location

0   miles   2

with rainbow trout.

Much of this park remains the realm of the experienced backcountry adventurer. Good map reading and navigational skills are required in the trailless wilderness areas, and only those experienced in glacial travel and crevasse rescue techniques should wander onto the glaciers and icefields of the high country.

Bear in mind that private cabins and property are found along the coast and in some interior locations, particularly around Halibut Cove, Sadie and Tutka bays, and China Poot Lake.

Contact the park office for cabin reservations or information on water and air taxi service to Kachemak Bay State Park or Kachemak Bay State Wilderness Park:

Division of Parks and Outdoor Recreation
Kachemak Bay State Park and State Wilderness Park
P. O. Box 3248
Homer, Alaska 99603
Telephone (907) 235-7024.

Kachemak Bay Hiking Trails

(summarized from Alaska State Parks)

The park trails are maintained by a volunteer trail crew during the summer. At times they receive little maintenance and often climb over steep, rugged, wet terrain. Routes may be hidden by fallen trees or tall grass. Exposed rocks and roots and wet, boggy areas are common. Be prepared to cross glacial streams. For up to date information, contact the park ranger in Homer or Halibut Cove Lagoon before your trip.

Grewingk Glacier

This is an easy hike over flat terrain through spruce and cotton-wood to the outwash of Grewingk Glacier. Views of the glacier and surrounding area are well worth the trip. Water taxis will usually drop you off at Right Beach where there is a small camping area. Note: Right Beach is accessible by foot only from the north and only at low tide. Access to the glacial ice from the trail or near the small lake at the terminus of the glacier is not advised; it is very hazardous to attempt access and many people have been injured attempting to do so.

Saddle Trail

This is a connecting trail that leads over the saddle between Halibut Cove and the Grewingk Glacier for access to the Alpine Ridge and Lagoon trails. It is steep on the Halibut Cove side.

Alpine Ridge

This steep hike begins from the high point on the Saddle Trail and follows a ridge up through spruce and alder stands to the alpine tundra. Once above timberline, the views of the Grewingk Glacier and glacial valleys are spectacular. Some rock cairns mark part of the trail.

Lagoon Trail

The Lagoon Trail is a long, rugged trail with many switchbacks and at least one creek crossing which can be difficult during high water. The trail connects the Saddle Trail to the China Poot Lake Trail at the Ranger Station along the east side of Halibut Cove Lagoon. Park rangers report that many people misjudge their hiking time for this trail; this trail takes experienced, well-conditioned hikers up to five hours to complete, one way, although it is only 5.5 miles in length.

Goat Rope Spur Trail

This short steep trail through alders begins at the highest point on the Lagoon Trail. It leads hikers up through a notch in the rocks to alpine areas.

China Poot Lake

This trail begins at Halibut Cove Lagoon and passes three lakes beneath China Poot Peak. You will pass through spruce forest and muskek most of the way.

Poot Peak

This steep, slick, unmaintained route begins across the China Poot Lake inlet stream bridge and heads up to timberline. Climbing the 2,100-foot peak is hazardous due to shifting scree and rotten rock. Hand and foot holds are poor at best, particularly so in wet weather. Hikers can experience excellent views of Wosnesenski Glacier and Kachemak Bay.

Wosnesenski Trail

The trail begins where it meets the China Poot Peak Trail, about 10 minutes after crossing the inlet stream bridge at China Poot Lake. This fairly easy trail winds along the shoreline of three lakes. Be careful if you decide to cross the river while exploring the valley. Water levels are highest in July and August.

KACHEMAK BAY STATE PARK HIKING TRAIL SUMMARY

Trail	Rating	Distance	Time
Alpine Ridge	moderate+	2.0	1.75
China Poot Lake	easy+	2.5	1.5
Goat Rope Spur	difficult	0.5	1.0
Grewingk Glacier	easy	3.5	1.5
Lagoon	moderate+	5.5	5.0
Poot Peak	difficult	2.0	2.0
Saddle Trail	moderate	1.0	0.5
Wosnesenski Trail	easy-mod	2.0	1.3

Distance is one way. Time assumes good physical condition and light day pack. Check with park rangers for local conditions and the latest trail information before leaving.

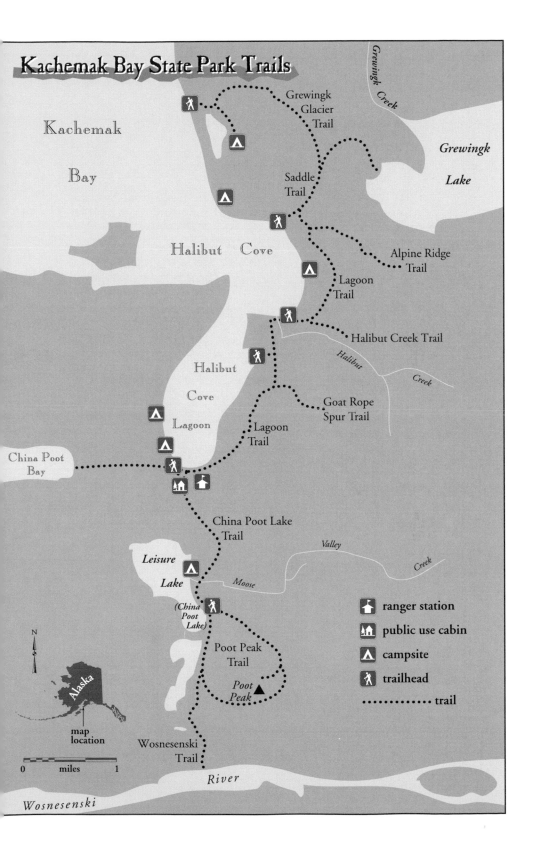

Kachemak Bay State Park Trails

Kachemak

Bay

Grewingk Creek

Grewingk
Glacier
Trail

Grewingk
Lake

Saddle
Trail

Halibut   Cove

Alpine Ridge
Trail

Lagoon
Trail

Halibut Creek Trail

Halibut

Creek

Halibut

Cove

Goat Rope
Spur Trail

Lagoon

Lagoon
Trail

China Poot
Bay

China Poot Lake
Trail

Valley

Creek

Leisure

Lake

Moose

(China
Poot
Lake)

Poot Peak
Trail

Poot
Peak

ranger station

public use cabin

campsite

trailhead

•••••••••• trail

N

Alaska

map
location

0   miles   1

Wosnesenski
Trail

River

Wosnesenski

APPENDIX 1

Checklist of Mammals of Kenai Fjords

Terrestrial Mammals

____ Bat, Little Brown	*Myotis lucifugus*
____ Bear, Black	*Ursus americanus*
____ Bear, Brown	*Ursus arctos*
____ Beaver	*Castor canadensis*
____ Coyote	*Canis latrans*
____ Goat, Mountain	*Oreamnos americanus*
____ Hare, Snowshoe	*Lepus americanus*
____ Lemming, Northern Bog	*Synaptomys borealis*
____ Lynx	*Lynx canadensi*
____ Marmot, Hoary	*Marmota caligata*
____ Marten	*Martes americana*
____ Mink	*Mustela vison*
____ Moose	*Alces alces*
____ Mouse, Meadow Jumping	*Zapus hudsonicus*
____ Otter, River	*Lutra canadensis*
____ Porcupine	*Erethizon dorsatum*
____ Shrew, Arctic	*Sorex arcticus*
____ Shrew, Dusky	*Sorex vagrans*
____ Shrew, Masked	*Sorex cinereus*
____ Shrew, Northern Water	
____ Shrew, Pygmy	
____ Squirrel, Red	*Tamiasciurus hudsonicus*
____ Vole, Alaska	*Microtus miurus*
____ Vole, Meadow	*Microtus pennsylvanicus*
____ Vole, Red-backed	*Clethrionomys rutilus*
____ Vole, Tundra	*Microtus oeconomus*
____ Weasel, Short-tailed	*Mustela erminea*
____ Wolf	*Canis lupus*
____ Wolverine	*Gulo gulo*

Possible Additions

Fox, Red	Vulpes vulpes
Lemming, Collared	Dicrostonyx torquatus
Muskrat	Ondotra zibethica
Pika, Collared	Ochotona collaris

_____ Squirrel, Arctic Ground   *Citelus parryii*
_____ Vole, Yellow-cheeked

Marine Mammals

_____ Orca   *Orcinus orca*
_____ Otter, Sea   *Enhydra lutris*
_____ Porpoise, Dall's   *Phocoenoides dalli*
_____ Porpoise, Harbor   *Phocoena phocoena*
_____ Sea Lion, Steller's   *Eumetopias jubatus*
_____ Seal, Harbor   *Phoca vitulina*
_____ Whale, Fin   *Balaenoptera physalus*
_____ Whale, Gray   *Eschrichtius robustus*
_____ Whale, Humpback   *Megaptera novaeangliae*
_____ Whale, Minke   *Balaenoptera acutorostrata*
_____ Whale, Sei   *Balaenoptera borealis*

Possible Additions

_____ Dolphin, Pacific White-sided   *Lagenorhynchus obliquidens*
_____ Seal, Northern Fur   *Collorhinus ursinus*
_____ Whale, Baird's Beaked   *Berardius bairdii*
_____ Whale, Beluga   *Delphinapterus leucas*
_____ Whale, Blue   *Balaenoptera musculus*

SELECTED LAND MAMMALS OF KENAI FJORDS

Black bears are common throughout Kenai Fjords, whereas brown bears are only occassionly sighted in the Exit Glacier/Resurrection River part of the park or in the Nuka River area. Black bears are can be distinguished from brown bears by their straight facial profile (the profile of a brown bear is dished or curved). They are opportunistic feeders and forage from tideline to upper alpine zone. Though they have been seen chasing goats and other mammals in the park, they rely most heavily on roots, berries and fish for food. Black bears are powerful animals that should be treated with respect.

Moose are found only in a few parts of the park. The Exit Glacier area is a favorite spot since the willow that they favor thrives here. They are also found in the Nuka Bay area, especially around Beauty Bay where they cross over the low Nuka River divide. Cows with calves are sometimes seen near Exit Glacier. Beware—these thousand-pound cows will vigorously defend their calves, so don't approach them. Fall and winter are the best times for spotting moose when the brushy thickets the inhabit are free of leaves.

Mountain Goat Mountain goats are right at home in the steep, rugged fjords. They are often confused with Dall sheep, but, though common in other parts of Alaska, Dall sheep do not occur regularly in Kenai Fjords National Park. Mountian goats favor high, steep meadows during the summer months. Loose bands of nannie-goats with kids are common on the cliffs around Exit Glacier.

River Otter River otters are commonly seen in the fjords in groups of two or more. They are not confined to fresh water and are often seen swimming in the ocean and foraging in the intertidal zone. They can be distinguished from sea otters by their long, round tails and their swimming style—river otters on their stomachs while sea otters almost always swim on their backs.

Wolverine Elusive is a word often used to describe wolverines. They are relatives of the mink, weasel, and river otter, and roam huge territories of hundreds of square miles. They are primarily carnivorous, feeding on snowshoe hares, ptarmigan, grouse, squirrels and carrion. Several sightings have been reported from the Aialik Bay Public Use Cabin area.

Other mammals in the park include beavers, porcupines, red squirrels, coyotes, wolves, marmots and lynx.

Selected Marine Mammals of the Kenai Fjords

Steller's Sea Lion These huge, brown mammals take their name from Georg W. Steller, the naturalist on Vitus Bering's voyage of discovery who first described them for science in 1741. They were well known to native Aleuts long before then, and were an important source of food, clothing and skins for covering kayaks. Largest of the eared seals, an average adult male weighs about 1,200 pounds. They feed on a variety of fishes, including pollock, salmon and herring. Breeding and pupping occurs in May, June and July, and most pups are produced at just a few large rookeries. The Chiswell Islands are a favored "haulout," or resting place, rather than a rookery.

Harbor Seal Harbor seals are a wide spread species, ranging throughout both the north Atlantic and Pacific Oceans. They are typically grey colored with dark or light splotches, and the average adult weighs about 180 pounds. Strong swimmers, they have been known to stay submerged for 20 minutes and dive up to 600 feet deep in pursuit of fish, octopus and squid. Pupping takes place in early June and is not concentrated at large rookeries, but occurs at haulouts throughout their range. Floating glacial ice is a favorite haulout and large numbers of harbor seals can be seen suckling their young near Aialik, Northwestern, and McCarty glaciers.

Sea Otter Smallest of all marine mammals, an average adult male weighs around 80 pounds. They are the only marine mammal known to use tools for feeding, often balancing a small rock on their chest which they use to crack open shellfish. They eat mussels, clams, sea urchins and a variety of other mollusks and crustaceans.

Dall's Porpoise These black and white porpoises are fast, powerful swimmers that show little fear of boats. Travelling in groups of five to twenty animals, they often intentionally approach moving vessels to ride the bow and stern waves, giving passengers a thrilling show. They feed on fish, squid and crustaceans and are sometimes preyed upon by orcas and large sharks.

Harbor Porpoise These shy, small porpoises inhabit calm coastal waters throughout the northern hemisphere. In the Kenai Fjords, they are more likely to be encountered by kayakers or quiet pleasure boaters than by the larger tour boats since they are so wary. Reaching just six feet in length, an average adult weighs just 100 pounds. A good look at them might reveal their light, mottled sides. Otherwise, they will simply appear dark grey.

Orca Also known as killer whales, orcas travel in groups of three to 50 called "pods." They communicate with each other with a language of underwater squeals and groans, and they locate prey by echolocation, emitting a series of clicks and interpreting the returning echoes. They bear a striking black-and-white pattern, but their most conspicuous feature is their large dorsal fin. Males may have a triangular black fin nearly six feet high. While many feed primarily on fish, some orcas are known to attack and kill seals, porpoises and even larger whales. The orcas of Kenai Fjords may also range to Prince William Sound and the waters around Kodiak Island.

Humpback Whale Humpbacks are present in Kenai Fjords only during the spring and summer, travelling thousands of miles to feed in the rich waters. They are baleen whales, filtering huge quantities of water through their mouths and trapping their prey in the close mesh of thin baleen plates. Usually seen alone or in groups of two or three, they have a habit of breaching, or leaping partially clear of the water, a spectacular display to witness. They are usually dark in color with long, white flippers, and have knobby bumps and protuberances on their heads and lower jaws. They may even have barnacles attached to them, tiny crustaceans hitching a free ride on these magnificent whales. Once a target of commercial whalers, humpbacks were hunted to the brink of extinction. Still endangered today, they are beginning a long, slow comeback under international protection.

Checklist of Selected Plants of Kenai Fjords

Apiaceae

_____ Beach Lovage   *Ligusticum scoticum*
_____ Cow Parsnip   *Heracleum lanatum*
_____ Sweet Cicely   *Asmorphiza purpurea*
_____ Wild Celery   *Angelica lucida*

Araceae (Arum Family)

_____ Skunk Cabbage   *Lysichiton americanum*

Araliaceae (Ginseng family)

_____ Devil's Club   *Echinopanax horridum*

Aspleniaceae (Lady Fern Family)

_____ Lady Fern   *Athyrium filix-femina*
_____ Fragile Fern   *Crystopteris fragilis*

Asteraceae (Composite Family)

_____ Siberian Aster   *Aster sibiricus*
_____ Douglas' Aster   *Aster subspicatus*
_____ Beach Grounsel   *Senecio pseudo-Arnica*
_____ Coastal Fleabane   *Erigeron peregrinu*
_____ Goldenrod   *Salidago multiradiata*
_____ Hawkweed   *Hieraceim triste*
_____ Pussytoes   *Antennaria monocephala*
_____ Rattlesnake Root   *Prenanthes alata*
_____ Sweet Coltsfoot   *Petasites brigidus*
_____ Yarrow   *Achillea borealis*

Betulaceae (Birch Family)

_____ Sitka Alder   *Alnus crispa*

Brassicaceae (Mustard Family)

_____ Rock Cress   *Arabis lyrata*
_____ Scurvy Grass   *Cochlearia officipalis*
_____ Winter Cress   *Barbarea orthoceras*
_____ Yellow Cress   *Rorippa islandica*

Boraginaceae

_____ Bluebell, Lungwort   *Mertensia paniculata*
_____ Forget-Me-Not   *Myosotis alpestris*
_____ Oysterleaf   *Mertensia maritimus*

Campanulaceae (Bluebell Family)
_____ Harebell, Bluebell   *Campanula rotundifolia*

Caprifoliaceae (Honeysuckle Family)
_____ Highbush Cranberry   *Viburum edule*
_____ Pacific Red Elder   *Sambucus racemosa*

Caryophyllaceae (Pink Family)
_____ Beach Grass   *Honckenya peploides*
_____ Chickweed   *Stellaria media*
_____ Moss Campion   *Silene acaulis*
_____ Canada Sandspurry   *Sperugularia canadensis*
_____ Sitka Starwort   *Stellaria sitchana*

Chenopodiaceae (Goosefoot Family)
_____ Pigweed   *Chenopodium album*

Cornaceae (Dogwood Family)
_____ Bunchberry, Dogwood   *Cornus canadensis*

Crassulaceae (Stonecrop Family)
_____ Roseroot   *Sedum rosea*

Cyperaceae (Sedge Family)
_____ Cotton Grass   *Eriophorum augustifolium*
_____ Sitka Sedge   *Carex sitchensis*
_____ Hoary Sedge   *Carex canescens*

Drosseraceae (Sundew Family)
_____ English Sundew   *Drosera anglica*
_____ Round Leaf Sundew   *Drosera rotundifolia*

Ericacea (Heath Family)
_____ Alaska Moss Heath   *Cassiope Stelleriana*
_____ Alpine Azalea   *Loiseleuria procumbans*
_____ Alpine Blueberry   *Vaccinium religinosum*
_____ Blueberry   *Vaccinium ovalfolium*
_____ Bog Rosemary   *Andromeda polifolia*
_____ Copper Flower   *Cladothamnus pyrolaeflorus*
_____ Cranberry   *Oxycoccus microcarpus*
_____ Dwarf Blueberry   *Vaccinium caespitosum*
_____ Mountain Heather   *Phyllodoce aleutica*

Equisetaceae (Horsetail Family)
_____ Water Horsetail   *Equisetum Fluviatile*
_____ Marsh Horsetail   *Equisetum palustre*
_____ Woodland Horsetail   *Equisetum silvaticum*

Gentianaceae (Gentian Family)
_____ Alpine Gentian   *Gentiana platypetala*
_____ Glaucous gentian   *Gentiana glauca*
_____ Star Gentian   *Swertia perennis*

Geraniaceae (Geranium Family)
_____ Cranesbill, Wild Geranium   *Geranium erianthum*

Iridaceae (Iris Family)
_____ Blue-Eyed Grass   *Sisyrinchum litorale*
_____ Wild Flag   *Iris setosa*

Junaceae (Rush Family)

_____   *Juncus Drummondii*

Juncaginaceae (Arrowgrass Family)
_____ Arrow grass   *Triglochin maritima*

Leguminosae (Pea Family)
_____ Alsike Clover   *Trifolium hybridum*
_____ Beach Pea   *Lathyrus maritimus*
_____ Milk Vetch   *Astragalus alpinus*
_____ Nootka Lupine   *Lupinus nootkatensis*

Lentibulariaceae (Bladderwort Family)
_____ Butterwort   *Pinguicula vulgaris*

Liliaceae (Lily Family)
_____ Choclate Lilly   *Fritillaria camschatcensis*
_____ False Asphodel   *Tofieldia coccinea*
_____ False Hellebore   *Veratrum viride*
_____ Twisted Stalk   *Streptopus amplexifolius*
_____ Wild Chive   *Allium schoenoprasum*

Lycopodiaceae (Club Moss Family)
_____ Alpine Club Moss   *Lycopodium alpinum*
_____ Common Club Moss   *Lycopodium clavatum*
_____ Fir Club Moss   *Lycopodium selago*
_____ Stiff Club Moss   *Lycopodium annotinum*

Nymphaeaceae (Water Lily Family)
_____ Yellow Pond Lily   *Nuphar polysepalum*

Onagraceae (Evening Primrose Family)
_____ Common Fireweed   *Epilobium augustifolium*
_____ Enchanter's Nightshade   *Ciricaea alpina*
_____ Pimpernel Willow-Herb   *Epilobium anagallidifolium*

_____ Slender-Fruited Willow Herb *Epilobium leptocarpum*
_____ River Beauty, Dwarf Fireweed *Epilobium latifolium*

Orchidaceae (Orchid Family)
  _____ Bog Orchid   *Platanthera dilatata*
  _____ Bog Orchid   *Platanthera convallariaefolia*
  _____ Heartleaf Twayblade   *Listera cordata*

Papaveraceae (Poppy Family)
  _____ Alaska Poppy   *Papaver alaskanum*
  _____ Pale Pink Poppy   *Papaver alboroseum*

Pinaceae (Pine Family)
  _____ Mountain Hemlock   *Tsuga mertensiana*
  _____ Sitka Spruce   *Picea sitchana*
  _____ Western Hemlock   *Tsuga heterophylla*

Plantaginaceae (Plantain Family)
  _____ Goosetongue   *Plantago maritima*

Primulaceae (Primrose Family)
  _____ Fen-Flowered Shooting Star *Dodecatheon pulchellum*
  _____ European Starflower   *Trientalis europaea*

Poaceae (Grass Family)
  _____ Alpine Holy Grass   *Hierochloe alpina*
  _____ Beach Rye Grass   *Elymus arenarius*
  _____ Bluegrass   *Poa alpina* (and other species)
  _____ Bluejoint   *Calamagrostis canadensis*
  _____ Mountain Timothy   *Phleum commutatum*
  _____ Red Fescue   *Festuco rubra*
  _____ Vanilla Grass   *Hierochloe odorata*

Polemoniaceae (Polemonium Family)
  _____ Jacob's Ladder   *Polemonium acutiflorum*

Polygonaceae (Buckwheat Family)
  _____ Mountain Sorrel   *Oyria digyna*
  _____   *Rumex fenestrtus*

Portulaceae (Purslane Family)
  _____ Spring Beauty   *Claytonia sibirica*

Pyrolacaea (Wintergreen Family)
  _____ Single Delight   *Moneses uniflora*
  _____ Pink Wintergreen   *Pyrola asarifolia*

Ranunculaceae (Crowfoot Family)

_____	Larkspur	*Delphinium glaucum*
_____	Marsh Marigold	*Caltha palustris*
_____	Monkshood	*Aconitum delphinifolium*
_____	Western Columbine	*Aquilegia formosa*

Rosaceae (Rose Family)

_____	Alaska Spirea	*Spiraea Beauverdiana*
_____	Large-Leaf Avens	*Geum macrophyllum*
_____	Cloudberry	*Rubus chamaemorus*
_____	Goatsbeard	*Aruncus sylvester*
_____		*Luetkea pectinata*
_____	Mountain Avens	*Dryas octopetala*
_____	Nagoonberry	*Rubus arcticus*
_____	Oregon Crab Apple	*Mulus fusca*
_____	Salmonberry	*Rubus spectabilis*
_____	Sitka Burnet	*Sanguisorba stipulata*
_____	Yellow Dryas	*Dryas Drummondii*

Salicaceae (Willow Family)

_____	Arctic Willow	*Salix arctica*
_____	Black Cottonwood	*Populus balsamifera*
_____	Feltleaf Willow	*Salix alaxensis*
_____	Sitka Willow	*Salix sitchensis*

Saxifragaceae (Saxifrage Family)

_____	Alpine Heuchera	*Heuchera glabra*
_____	Bog Star	*Parnassia palustris*
_____	Coast Saxifrage	*Saxifraga ferruginea*
_____	Lace Flower	*Tiarella trifoliata*
_____	Northern Black Currant	*Ribes hudsonianum*
_____	Red-stemmed Saxifrage	*Saxifraga Lyallii*
_____	Spotted Saxifrage	*Saxifraga bronchialis*
_____	Trailing Black Currant	*Ribes laxiflorum*
_____	Tufted Saxifrage	*Saxifraga caespitosa*

Scrophulariaceae (Figwort Family)

_____	Lousewort	*Pedicularis verticillata*
_____	Yellow Indian Paintbrush	*Castelleja unalaschensis*
_____	Yellow Monkey Flower	*Mimulus guttatus*

Selaginaceae (Spikemoss Family)

_____	Spike Moss	*Selaginella selaginoides*

Urticaceae (Nettle Family)

_____	Nettle	*Uritica gracilis*
_____	Lyall Nettle	*Uritica lylalli*

Valerianaceae (Valerian Family)
_____ Capitate Valerian   *Valeriana capitata*

Violaceae (Violet Family)
_____ Marsh Violet   *Viola epipsila*

SELECTED WILDFLOWER DESCRIPTIONS

Beach Pea *(Lathyrus maritimus)* Sprawling mats of beach pea can be found on many of the rocky beaches in the fjords. The blossoms are bluish-violet and most prominent from late May to late June. Look for bees busily gathering pollen from them on warm afternoons.

Cow Parsnip *(Heracleum lanatum)* Cow parsnip is found in coastal meadows, woodlands, and alpine areas, and can grow to eight feet tall. The leaves are large, broad, and hairy, and the stems of the plant are hollow. Clusters of white blossoms appear from July to mid-August and attract flies and other insects. Beware—some people experience an allergic skin reaction to cow parsnip which results in a burning rash and blisters.

Chocolate Lilly *(Fritillaria camschatcensis)* This brown-flowered perennial grows in damp woodlands and meadows throughout Southcentral Alaska. Its somewhat unpleasant odor has earned it the nickname "skunk lily." Look for blossoms from mid-June to mid-July.

Dogwood *(Cornus canadensis)* Also known as "Bunchberry," these low growing plants occur commonly on the shady floor of the spruce/hemlock forests. What appears to be a single white blossom is actually a cluster of tiny flowers set off by four white sepals. They bloom in June and July, and transform into a tight bunch of reddish-orange berries in August.

Dwarf Fireweed *(Epilobium latifolium)* This small version of fireweed is sometimes called "river beauty" since it grows commonly along river bars or other gravelly areas. It grows to about twenty inches tall and has purplish-pink blossoms. Look for it blooming in July and August along the streams at Exit Glacier. Its taller cousin, common fireweed, also occurs in the park.

Wild Geranium *(Geranium erianthum)* Wild geraniums grow to over two feet tall and have delicate, pale lavender blossoms. They can be found seen in bloom from late June through August and are common along portions of the Harding Icefield Trail.

Yellow Monkeyflower *(Mimulus guttatus)* These bright yellow flowers are sometimes called wild snapdragon, and can be be found growing along the moist, rocky slopes of the lower Harding Icefield Trail. Look closely at the blossoms to see the reddish spots that help attract pollinating insects.

Yellow Dryas *(Dryas Drummondii)* Mats of dryas occur commonly in dry, gravelly, disturbed areas, including areas recently feed from glacial ice. In June and early July, the nodding blossoms can be found in the Exit Glacier area. Later in the season, the flowers are replaced by a fluffy white seed head.

Checklist of Birds of Kenai Fjords

Gaviidae
____ Red-throated Loon
____ Pacific Loon
____ Common Loon
____ Yellow-billed Loon

Podicipedidae
____ Horned Grebe
____ Red-necked Grebe

Procellariidae
____ Northern Fulmar
____ Sooty Shearwater
____ Short-tailed Shearwater
____ Pink-footed Shearwater

Hydrobatidae
____ Leach's Storm Petrel
____ Fork-tailed Storm Petrel

Phalacrocoracidae
____ Double-crested Cormorant
____ Pelagic Cormorant
____ Red-faced Cormorant

Ardeidae
____ Great Blue Heron

Gruidae
____ Sandhill Crane

Anatidae
____ Tundra Swan
____ Trumpeter Swan
____ Greater White-fronted Goose
____ Snow Goose
____ Brant
____ Canada Goose

____ Green-winged Teal
____ Mallard
____ Northern Pintail
____ Blue-winged Teal
____ Northern Shoveler
____ Gadwall
____ Eurasion Wigeon
____ American Wigeon
____ Canvasback
____ Greater Scaup
____ Lesser Scaup
____ Common Eider
____ King Eider
____ Steller's Eider
____ Harlequin Duck
____ Oldsquaw
____ Black Scoter
____ Surf Scoter
____ White-winged Scoter
____ Common Goldeneye
____ Barrow's Goldeneye
____ Bufflehead
____ Hooded Merganser
____ Common Merganser
____ Red-breasted Merganser

Haematopodidae
____ Black Oystercatcher

Charadriidae
____ Black-bellied Plover
____ Lesser Golden Plover
____ Semipalmated Plover
____ Killdeer

Scolopacidae
_____ Greater Yellowlegs
_____ Lesser Yellowlegs
_____ Solitary Sandpiper
_____ Wandering Tattler
_____ Spotted Sandpiper
_____ Whimbrel
_____ Hudsonian Godwit
_____ Ruddy Turnstone
_____ Black Turnstone
_____ Surfbird
_____ Semipalmated Sandpiper
_____ Western Sandpiper
_____ Least Sandpiper
_____ Pectoral Sandpiper
_____ Rock Sandpiper
_____ Dunlin
_____ Short-billed Dowitcher
_____ Long-billed Dowitcher
_____ Common Snipe
_____ Red-necked Phalarope
_____ Red Phalarope

Laridae
_____ Pomarine Jaeger
_____ Parasitic Jaeger
_____ Long-tailed Jaeger
_____ Bonaparte's Gull
_____ Mew Gull
_____ Ring-billed Gull
_____ Herring Gull
_____ Thayer's Gull
_____ Glaucous-winged Gull
_____ Glaucous Gull
_____ Black-legged Kittiwake
_____ Sabine's Gull
_____ Arctic Tern
_____ Aleutian Tern

Accipitridae
_____ Osprey
_____ Bald Eagle
_____ Northern Harrier

_____ Sharp-shinned Hawk
_____ Northern Goshawk
_____ Red-tailed Hawk
_____ Rough-legged Hawk
_____ Golden Eagle

Falconidae
_____ Merlin
_____ Peregrine Falcon
_____ Gyrfalcon

Phasianidae
_____ Spruce Grouse
_____ Willow Ptarmigan
_____ Rock Ptarmigan
_____ White-tailed Ptarmigan

Columbidae
_____ Rock Dove

Strigidae
_____ Short-eared Owl
_____ Great Horned Owl
_____ Great Gray Owl
_____ Snowy Owl
_____ Northern Hawk-Owl
_____ Northern Saw-whet Owl
_____ Boreal Owl
_____ Western Screech Owl

Trochilidae
_____ Rufous Hummingbird

Alcedinidae
_____ Belted Kingfisher

Picidae
_____ Downy Woodpecker
_____ Hairy Woodpecker
_____ Three-toed Woodpecker
_____ Northern Flicker

Tyrannidae
____ Olive-sided Flycatcher
____ Western Wood-Pewee
____ Say's Phoebe
____ Alder Flycatcher

Alaudidae
____ Horned Lark

Hirundinidae
____ Tree Swallow
____ Violet-green Swallow
____ Bank Swallow
____ Cliff Swallow

Corvidae
____ Gray Jay
____ Steller's Jay
____ Black-billed Magpie
____ Northwestern Crow
____ Common Raven

Paridae
____ Black-capped Chickadee
____ Boreal Chickadee
____ Chestnut-backed Chickadee

Certhiidae
____ Brown Creeper

Troglodytidae
____ Winter Wren

Muscicapidae
____ Golden-crowned Kinglet
____ Ruby-crowned Kinglet
____ Grey-cheeked Thrush
____ Swainson's Thrush
____ Hermit Thrush
____ American Robin
____ Varied Thrush
____ Northern Wheatear

Laniidae
____ Northern Shrike

Motacillidae
____ Water Pipit

Cinclidae
____ American Dipper

Bombycillidae
____ Bohemian Waxwing

Sturnidae
____ European Starling

Emberizidae
____ Orange-crowned Warbler
____ Yellow Warbler
____ Yellow-rumped Warbler
____ Townsend's Warbler
____ Blackpoll Warbler
____ Northern Waterthrush
____ Wilson's Warbler
____ American Tree Sparrow
____ Savannah Sparrow
____ Fox Sparrow
____ Song Sparrow
____ Lincoln's Sparrow
____ White-throated Sparrow
____ Dark-eyed Junco
____ Lapland Longspur
____ Snow Bunting
____ Rusty Blackbird

Fringillidae
____ Rosy Finch
____ Pine Grosbeak
____ Red Crossbill
____ White-winged Crossbill
____ Common Redpoll
____ Hoary Redpoll
____ Pine Siskin

Selected Seabirds of Kenai Fjords and the Chiswell Islands

Black-Legged Kittiwake These small gull-like birds nest in huge, noisy colonies in the Chiswell Islands. As the name implies, their legs and feet are black. Their wing tips are also solid black, as if they have been dipped in a pot of ink. Look for them plunging from the sky into the sea to catch small fish or swarming near their nesting cliffs.

Common Murre These black-and-white seabirds gather in huge numbers and crowd close together on steep cliffs to nest. They lay their single egg on bare rock. The eggs are pear-shaped so that, if disturbed, they will roll around in a circle instead of rolling off the edge of the cliff. Murres are strong divers and have reportedly been caught in fishing nets three hundred feet deep. Their close cousin, the thick-billed murre, can be regularly spotted in the Chiswell Islands by careful observers. They are distinguished by a blacker head, a sharp point where the white breast meets the black throat, and a white stripe along the edge of their bill.

Parakeet Auklet Smaller than rhinoceros auklets, parakeet auklets have a small, red, upturned bill and just one white plume behind each eye. Their nests, deep in natural rock crevices, are difficult to detect. Like the rhinoceros auklets, they only approach their nests at night. Parakeet Auklets have a small pouch beneath their tongue in which they store food to take to their young.

Horned Puffins Colorful, cute and clownish with their orange feet, white breasts, and red and yellow bills, horned puffins are a favorite with visitors to the fjords. Their name refers to the small "horn" of fleshy tissue just above their eyes. These birds nest in natural crevices or holes in cliffs and rockslides. In July and August, watch for shiny silver fish hanging from their beaks as they fly back to their nests to feed their young. Small spines and grooves on the roof of the mouth and top of the tongue aid the puffin in holding on to its slippery prey.

Tufted Puffins These cousins of the horned puffin are also clownish-looking with their orange bills, orange feet and yellow tufts. They nest in deep burrows which they dig in the soil near the tops of islands or bluffs, often returning to the exact same burrow year after year. Like all puffins, they spend most of their lives at sea, remaining far from land for up to eight months. These heavy-bodied birds require long running takeoffs into the wind. They sometimes get so full of fish that they are too heavy to take off at all.

Rhinoceros Auklet These birds are often seen in Aialik Bay near the entrance to Holgate Arm. Their name comes from the unusual yellow horn at the base of their bills. A close look also reveals two stripes of white plumes on each side of their heads. Their nesting behavior is secretive and their colonies difficult to detect since they only leave and enter their nest burrows at night.

BIBLIOGRAPHY

Andrews, Clarence L., *The Story of Alaska*, The Caxton Printers, Ltd., 1938.

Barry, Mary J. A., *History of Mining on the Kenai Peninsula*, Anchorage: Alaska Northwest Publishing Company, 1973.

_____, *Seward, Alaska, A History of the Gateway City*, Vol. 1, 1986.

_____, *Seward, Alaska, A History of the Gateway City*, Vol. 2, 1993.

Betts, Wooley, Mobley, et al., *Site Protection and Oil Spill Treatment at SEL-188*, Exxon Shipping Company, 1991.

Carefoot, Thomas, *Pacific Seashores, A Guide to Intertidal Ecology*, University of Washington Press, 1977

Davidson, Art, *In the Wake of the Exxon Valdez*, Sierra Club Books, 1990.

De Laguna, Frederica, *The Archaeology of Cook Inlet, Alaska*, The Alaska Historical Society, 1975.

Chugach Prehistory, University of Washington, 1956.

Follows, Donald S., Kenai Fjords National Park *in* Geology of National Parks, Fourth Edition, Kendall/Hunt Publishing Company, 1990.

Guide to the Geology of the Resurrection Bay-Eastern Kenai Fjords Area, edited by Steven Nelson and Thomas Hamilton, Anchorage: Alaska Geological Society.Grant, U.S. and Higgins, D.F., *Coastal Glaciers of Prince William Sound and Kenai Peninsula, Alaska*, USGS Bulletin #526, 1913.

Haggarty, Wooley, Erlandson and Crowell, *The 1990 Exxon Cultural Resource Program*, Exxon Shipping Company, 1991.

Hughes, Royston C., *Harding Icefield-Kenai Fjords National Monument Final Environmental Statement*, U.S. Dept. of the Interior, 1974.

Hulten, Eric, *Flora of Alaska and Neighboring Territories*, Stanford University Press, 1968.

Hunter, Celia and Wood, Ginny, *Alaska National Interest Lands*, The Alaska Geographic Society, Volume 8, Number 4, 1981.

Kozloff, Eugene M., *Seashore Life of the Northern Pacific Coast*, University of Washington Press, 1973.

Lockley, Ronald M. and Hosking, Eric, *Seabirds of the World*, Facts On File Publications, 1983.

Miller, Kathy Ann and Huggins, David O., *Pre- and Post-Oil Intertidal Biological Assessments in Kenai Fjords National Park*, NPS Files, 1990.

Mobely, Haggarty, Utermohle et al., *The 1989 Exxon Valdez Cultural Resource Program*, Exxon Shipping Company, 1990.

Nance, John J., *On Shaky Ground*, Wm. Morrow and Company, 1988.

Orth, Donald J., *Dictionary of Alaska Place Names*, Geological Survey Professional Paper 567, U.S. Department of the Interior, 1967.

Petroff, Ivan, *Report on the Population, Industries, and Resources of Alaska*, U. S. Dept. of the Interior, Census Office, 1884.

Rice, Bud, *Changes in the Harding Icefield, Kenai Peninsula*, Alaska, unpublished Masters thesis, 1987.

Sharp, Robert P., *Living Ice, Understanding Glaciers and Glaciation*, Cambridge University Press, 1988.

Strahler, Arthur, *Introduction to Physical Geography*, New York: John Wiley and Sons, Inc., 1965.

Stromsem, Nancy E., *A Guide To Alaskan Seabirds*, Alaska Natural History Association, 1982.

Teben'kov, M.D., *Atlas of the Northwest Coasts of America*, translated and edited by R.A. Pierce, The Limestone Press, 1981.

Trover, Ellen Lloyd, editor, *Alaska, A chronology and Documentary Handbook*, Ocean Publications, 1972.

Viereck, Leslie A., *Alaska Trees and Shrubs*, U.S. Department of Agriculture, 1972.

Wiles, Gregory C., *Holocene Fluctuations in the Southern Kenai Mountains, Alaska*, unpublished Phd. thesis, 1992.

Zwinger, Ann H. and Willard, Beatrice E., *Land Above the Trees: A Guide to American Alpine Tundra*, Harper and Row, 1972.

RECOMMENDED FURTHER READING

Davidson, Art, *In the Wake of the Exxon Valdez, the Devastating Impact of the Alaska Oil Spill*, Sierra Club Books, 1990.

Chevigny, Hector, *Russian America, The Great Alaskan Venture 1741-1867*, Binford and Mort, 1965.

Chevigny, Hector, *Lord of Alaska, The Story of Baranov and the Russian Adventure*, Binfords and Mort, 1971.

Dowd, John, *Sea Kayaking, A Manual for Long Distance Touring*, Seattle: University of Washington Press, 1981.

Hoyt, Erich, *Orca, The Whale Called Killer.*

Intertidal Bivalves, A guide to the Common Bivalves of Alaska, University of Alaska Press, 1991.

Kent, Rockwell, *Wilderness, A Journal of Quiet Adventure*, originally published by Leetes Island Books, 1920, now reprinted by various publishers.

Pratt, Verna E., *Field Guide to Alaskan Wildflowers*, Anchorage: Alaskakrafts Publishing, 1989.

Spencer, Page, *White Silk and Black Tar, A Journal of the Alaska Oil Spill*, Bergamot Books, 1990.

Washburne, Randall, *The Coastal Kayakers Manual*, The Globe Pequot Press, 1989.

Where Moutains Meet the Sea: Alaska's Gulf Coast, in *Alaska Geographic*, Volume 13, Number 3, 1986.